D1881648

THE HERITAGE OF INDIA SERIES (12)

A HISTORY OF URDU LITERATURE

THE HERITAGE OF INDIA SERIES (12)

A HISTORY OF URDU LITERATURE

BY

T. GRAHAME BAILEY, D.Litt., B.D., M. A.

GYAN

Published by

GYAN

Gyan Publishing House
5, Ansari Road
Daryaganj, New Delhi-110002
Phone: 011-47034999, 9811692060
E-mail: books@gyanbooks.com

Distribution Network
gyanbooks.com
India, USA, Canada, UK, Australia, France

ISBN: 978-81-212-8266-6 (PB)
First Published, 1932

2nd Impression 2023

Printed at: Gyan Press, Delhi.

THE HERITAGE OF INDIA SERIES (12); A HISTORY OF URDU LITERATURE

Author: T. GRAHAME BAILEY

EDITORIAL PREFACE

> Finally, brethren, whatsoever things are true, whatsoever things are honourable, whatsoever things are just, whatsoever things are pure, whatsoever things are lovely, whatsoever things are of good report; if there be any virtue, and if there be any praise, think on these things.

No section of the population of India can afford to neglect her ancient heritage. The treasures of knowledge, wisdom, and beauty which are contained in her literature, philosophy, art, and regulated life are too precious to be lost. Every citizen of India needs to use them, if he is to be a cultured modern Indian. This is as true of the Christian, the Muslim, the Zoroastrian as of the Hindu. But, while the heritage of India has been largely explored by scholars, and the results of their toil are laid out for us in books, they cannot be said to be really available for the ordinary man. The volumes are in most cases expensive, and are often technical and difficult. Hence this series of cheap books has been planned by a group of Christian men, in order that every educated Indian, whether rich or poor, may be able to find his way into the treasures of India's past. Many Europeans, both in India and elsewhere, will doubtless be glad to use the series.

The utmost care is being taken by the General Editors in selecting writers, and in passing manuscripts for the press. To every book two tests are rigidly applied: everything must be scholarly, and everything must be sympathetic. The purpose is to bring the best out of the ancient treasuries, so that it may be known, enjoyed, and used.

'THE ADORATION OF THE CHRIST-CHILD.'

(An Indian painting of the seventeenth century A.D., in the Freer Gallery of Art, Washington, D.C.)

THE HERITAGE OF INDIA SERIES

A HISTORY OF URDU LITERATURE

BY

T. GRAHAME BAILEY, D.Litt., B.D., M.A.

READER IN HINDI AND URDU IN THE UNIVERSITY OF LONDON;
FORMERLY MISSIONARY OF THE CHURCH OF SCOTLAND;

AUTHOR OF
A Grammar of the Shina Language; Linguistic Studies from the Himalayas; Languages of the Northern Himalayas; A Kanaurī Vocabulary; A Panjabi Phonetic Reader; A Brief Panjabi Grammar; An English-Panjabi Vocabulary; Panjabi Manual and Grammar (jointly)

ASSOCIATION PRESS
(Y.M.C.A.)
5 RUSSELL STREET, CALCUTTA

LONDON: OXFORD UNIVERSITY PRESS
NEW YORK, TORONTO, MELBOURNE
BOMBAY, CALCUTTA & MADRAS
1932

PRINTED IN INDIA
AT THE WESLEYAN MISSION PRESS
MYSORE CITY

PREFACE

THIS short history of Urdu Literature, completed in 1929, aims at describing Urdu and its literature down to the end of 1928. All writers who were alive then are excluded. The only living author to whom detailed reference has been made is Iqbāl, whose fame seems to warrant his inclusion.

The Bibliography shows what books are available for further study; there is very little in English.

The following are special features of this work:

(*a*) The views on the origin and early history of Urdu differ greatly from those of previous authors, particularly in the antiquity attributed to it and the importance attached to Panjabi and the Panjab in connection with its development. The remarks on the problem of the name 'Urdu' are new, and in explanation of the term 'Khaṛi Boli' I have tried incidentally to correct prevailing misconceptions on the subject.

(*b*) Much of what has been said about the Deccan and Dakhni writers is new. The place of the Deccan in Urdu literature has not been fully understood, and many Dakhni authors are unknown even by name to people who live in the north of India. I have therefore endeavoured to make this section as full as possible, hoping that the mention of these little-known or unknown names will not only induce students to read Dakhni works already in print, but lead to the publication of those at present in MS., and to the study of the valuable material contained in them.

(*c*) New information has been given too about Tahsin's

Nau Ṭarz i Muraṣṣa', Mīr Amman's *Bāg o Bahār*, and Amīr Khusrau's supposed work *Cahār Darvesh.*

I would draw the attention of readers to certain points:

(i) Many authors are repeatedly referred to; the fullest treatment will be found at the place first mentioned in the Index of Persons, i.e. according to the consecutive number of each. Thus, 'Naẓīr, Valī M., of Āgra, No. 125: 4, 20, 32, 41, 42, 98, 100.' Here the account of Naẓīr is given under No. 125.

(ii) Names of persons and works, Urdu words, and nearly all names of places are spelt with full diacritical marks. A few well-known words, chiefly place-names, are printed in their usual forms, or in some cases first with diacritical and subsequently without. They are those in the subjoined list:

Āgra	Marāṭhā
Deccan (Dakhan)	Marāṭhī
Delhi (Dihlī)	Oudh (Avadh)
Gujrāt	Panjāb
Gujrātī	Panjābī
Hindī	Paṭnā
Lahore (Lāhaur)	Turkī, Turkistān
Lucknow (Lakhnaū)	Urdū

(iii) The majority of Urdu authors have called their works by Arabic names. I have transliterated most of these with Arabic vocalisation, but in a few cases have treated them as if they were Urdu.

(iv) The system of transliteration of Urdu words is that of the Royal Asiatic Society, except for 'sh' and 'ng,' which I have allowed to stand without special marks, and n̲ to indicate a preceding nasal vowel. I have been unable to use the usual *tilde*, as the press did not possess it. A list of signs will be found on p. 108.

(v) The words 'religion' and 'religious' usually refer to Islām. Sometimes, as will be clear from the context, religion in general is intended.

(vi) The word 'Mugal' is employed in the usual conventional sense. The so-called Mugal emperors of India, Babur and his descendants, were actually Barlās Turks.

In order to give an idea of Urdu poetry I have inserted translations of seven poems. These are all my own. Most of them have appeared in the *Bulletin of the School of Oriental Studies*, and I am under obligation to the Editor of that Journal for permission to print them here.

I wish to express my thanks to an old student of my own, Dr. Mohiuddin Qadri, of the Osmaniya University, for having read all the proofs of the volume and made valuable suggestions.

T. GRAHAME BAILEY.

London,
April, 1932.

ADDENDA

1. Page 7. The relationship of father, son, and grandson, said on p. 17 to have existed between Nos. 5, 6 and 8 (Shāh Mīrā Jī, Shāh Burhān and Amīn ud Dīn A'lā), is according to popular report. Obviously one or two generations have dropped out.

2. On page 79, No. 184, line 1, for 'Urdu verse' read 'Urdu prose.' Āzād is the sole source of information about Saudā's prose, and his statements lack confirmation.

3. Page 60. Gālib probably did not hold the opinion attributed to him on p. 60. His phraseology is, however, sometimes like that of Lucknow writers.

CONTENTS

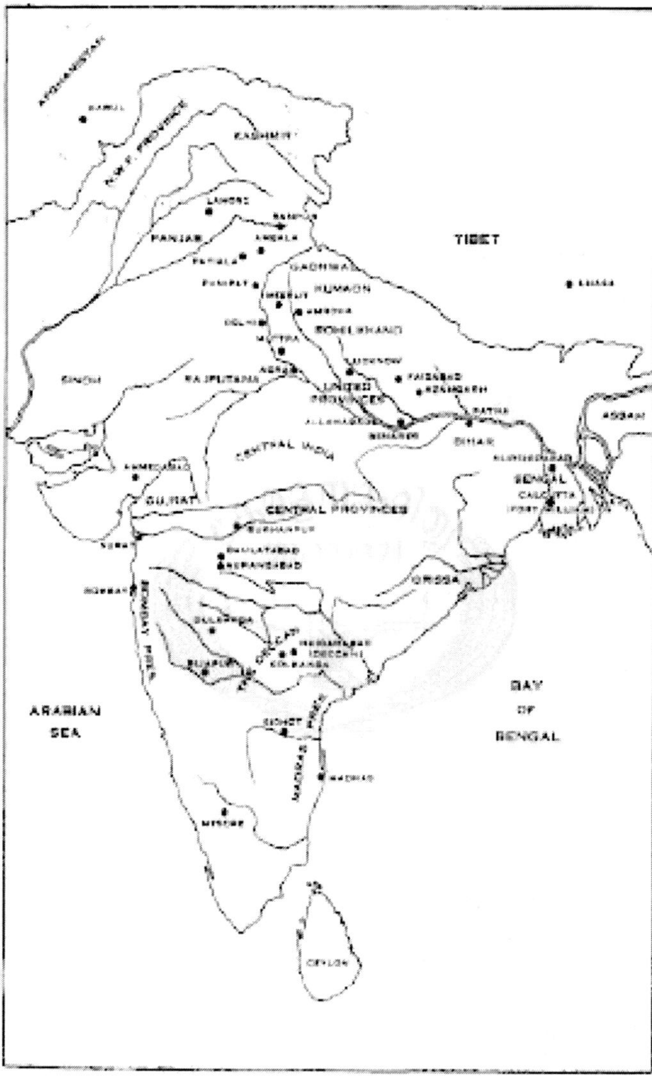

SKETCH-MAP

To illustrate the chief places in India connected with the history of Urdu Literature

INTRODUCTION

INFORMATION about the early Urdū poets is ultimately derived from old Persian anthologies, the great majority of which are unpublished. The earliest known are *Nikāt ush Shu'arā* by Mīr (1752), and *Tażkira e Gurdezī* (1752). Other famous anthologies are *Makhzan i Nikāt* by Qāim (1754); *Gulzār i Ibrāhīm* by 'Alī Ibrāhīm Khān Khalīl (1783); *Tażkira e Hasan* by Mīr Hasan (1776); *Tażkira e Shu'arā e Hindī* by Mushafī (1794). The first anthology in Urdu is 'Alī Lutf's *Gulshan i Hind* (1801).

There are several special difficulties in the study of Urdu literature:

1. Very little early literature has been published. Thus, the extant poetry written before 1800 is nearly all in MS. If we except Valī, Saudā, Mīr, Dard and Qāim, all the writers whose works have been published with any completeness were men who lived till after 1825. Many published works, especially those which were first printed in magazines, are not now obtainable.

2. It is often impossible to get access to original MSS., and we have to depend upon quotations in books. The anthologies are often inaccurate and their information is meagre. This accounts for the similarity between the various remarks made by modern authors about old writers; their authorities are the same.

3. There is considerable doubt about dates, particularly the earlier ones. The anthologies frequently omit dates, and often differ in the dates they give.

4. It is nearly impossible to be sure of the genuineness of early Urdu poetry.

Libraries in Great Britain and in some of the Feudatory States of India possess important Urdu MSS.; if these could be published, most of our problems would be solved.

Urdu Metre depends on quantity, not accent. Compared with Greek or Latin it has a fondness for long syllables. Thus among the commonest metres are

⏑ – – – / ⏑ – – – / ⏑ – – – / ⏑ – – /
and – ⏑ – – / – ⏑ – – / – ⏑ – – / – ⏑ – /
and ⏑ – – / ⏑ – – / ⏑ – – / ⏑ – /.

The Principal Forms of Urdu Poetry are:

Gazal, usually a short love lyric, sometimes a poem on a general subject. Strictly speaking it should have the same rhyme throughout. Urdu gazals are for the most part artificial and conventional.

Qaṣīda, a kind of ode, often a panegyric on a benefactor, sometimes a satire, sometimes a poem dealing with an important event. As a rule it is longer than the gazal, but it follows the same system of rhyme.

Marṣiya or elegy, nearly always on the death of Ḥasan, Ḥusain and their families, but occasionally on the death of relatives and friends. It is usually in six-lined stanzas with the rhyme *aaaabb*. The recitation of these elegies in the first ten days of Muḥarram is one of the great events in Muslim life. A fully developed marṣiya is almost an epic.

Maṣnavī, in the majority of cases a poetical romance. It may extend to several thousand lines, but generally is much shorter. A few maṣnavīs deal with ordinary domestic and other occurrences. Mīr and Saudā wrote some of this kind. They are always in heroic couplets, and the commonest metre is bacchic tetrameter with an iambus for the last foot, ⏑ – – / ⏑ – – / ⏑ – – / ⏑ – /.

Taẕkira, biographical anthology, almost always of poetry alone. This is often a mere collection of names with a line or two of information about each poet, followed by a specimen of his composition. On the other hand it may be a history of Urdu poetry with copious illustrative extracts. There are no really good taẕkiras. The best give biographical details, but fail in literary criticism, and we get little idea of style or poetical power, still less of the contents of poems. Even the large anthologies do not systematically review an author's work. Most of them have the names in alphabetical order, but one or two prefer the historical order. The majority quote only lyrics, and the quotations, usually chosen at random, do not really illustrate the poetry.

Dīwān, a collection of poems, chiefly gazals.

Kulliyāt, literally a complete collection of poems, but often applied to any collection containing poems of various kinds. Thus Akbar Ilāhābādī published three kulliyāts.

Takhallus, the name under which a poet writes. Every Urdu poet takes a special name by which he is generally known. It is introduced into the last line of all his gazals. Sometimes it is part of his personal name. Thus in the case of the poets Babar 'Alī Anīs and Salāmat 'Alī Dabīr, *Anīs* and *Dabīr* are the takhallus. Examples of poets using part of their ordinary names are Mīr Taqī Mīr and Mīr Hasan Hasan.

In order to avoid unnecessary Urdu terms in the text, certain English words have been used with a particular sense except where the context requires another. Thus:

Lyric (*or* love lyric)	= Gazal
Ode	= Qasīda
Elegy	= Marsiya
Romance (*or* poetical romance)	= Masnavī
Anthology (*or* biographical anthology)	= Tazkira

Rekhta is a Persian word meaning 'poured.' In Persia it has no literary significance, but in India it was used for the Urdu literary language, i.e. the language of poetry, or for Urdu poetry itself. Often it had the sense of gazal or couplet in a gazal. In the time of Nāsikh, d. 1838, Lucknow poets gave up the word rekhta and began to use 'Urdū' for the language, and 'gazal,' a word occasionally found in the eighteenth century, for the poem. In Delhi rekhta continued in use down to the Mutiny. Various explanations of rekhta are given.

1. It meant 'verse in two languages,' *e.g.* one line Persian and one Arabic, or one Persian and one Urdu. The earliest verse in north India was sometimes of this kind and was called rekhta. The name once given remained.

2. It meant 'fallen,' and Urdū, supposed to be fallen and worthless, received the name.

3. Urdū was called rekhta because it consisted of Hindi into which Arabic and Persian words had been *poured*.

4. It is a musical term introduced by Amīr Khusrau to mean a harmonising of Hindi words with Persian melodies.

5. It means a wall firmly constructed of different materials, as Urdū is of diverse linguistic elements. This is the opposite of (2).

The Most Important Urdu Poets. Urdu poetry is such a maze, that a useful purpose may be served if the leading poets are indicated. There will be diversity of opinion about such a list, for people differ in temperament and in attitude towards modern thought. No finality is claimed for the views here expressed, but they may be a guide. The names of poets from the Deccan may occasion surprise, for their greatness is not realised in north India. The old *tazkira* writers say little about them and only Valī is generally known.

1. THE GREATEST POETS. The groups are in order of rank, the names within each group in order of date. (*a*) Mīr, Gālib, Anīs. (*b*) Valī, Saudā, Nazīr of Agra, Iqbāl. (*c*) Dard, Mīr Ḥasan, Dāg, Ḥālī, Akbar.

2. THE BEST GAZAL WRITERS in order: Mīr, Valī, Dard, Gālib, Muṣḥafī, Ātish, Dāg, Amīr Mīnāī.

3. THE BEST QAṢĪDA WRITERS in order: Saudā, Zauq, Nuṣratī.

4. THE BEST MARSIYA WRITERS in order: Anīs, Dabīr, Mūnis, Khalīq, Zamīr; and the Dakhnī writers Hāshim 'Alī, Mirzā.

5. THE BEST MASNAVĪ WRITERS in order: Mīr Ḥasan, Asar, Mīr, Nasīm, Mūmin, and the Dakhnī writers Gavvāṣī, Nuṣratī, Ṭab'ī, Vajhī.

6. POETS WHO EXCELLED IN GENERAL POETRY in order of date: King Qulī Quṭb Shāh, Nazīr of Agra, Ḥālī, Akbar, Kaifī of the Deccan, Iqbāl. During the past 50 years perhaps the best, apart from poets already mentioned, have been Āzād, Jalāl, Taslīm, Ismā'īl, Shād.

The greatest poem of the last 100 years is probably Ḥālī's *Musaddas*, unless we regard Anīs's Elegies as one poem.

I

THE HISTORY OF URDU

How Urdu Began. Much has been written on the origin of Urdū. The word 'urdu' itself is Turkish and means 'army' or 'camp'; our English 'horde' is said to be connected with it. The Muslim army stationed in Delhi from 1193 onwards was known as *the Urdū* or *Urdū e Mu'allā*, the Exalted Army. It is usually believed that while this army spoke Persian, the inhabitants of the city spoke the Braj dialect of Hindi. There is no reason however to think that Braj was ever the language of Delhi. The people of the capital spoke an early variety of that form of Hindi now known as Khaṛī Bolī,[1] which is employed to-day in all Hindi prose and in most Hindi poetry. The idea that the army spoke Persian also requires reconsideration.

Mahmūd of Gaznī annexed the Panjab in 1027 and settled his army of occupation in Lahore. The famous scholar, Alberuni of Khivā (973–1048) lived there for some time while he studied Sanskrit and prosecuted his researches into Hinduism. Mahmūd's descendants held the Panjab till 1187, when they were defeated by their hereditary foes under Muhammad Gorī who had already sacked Gaznī. The first sultan of Delhi was Quṭb ud Dīn Aibak, a native of Turkistan, but a servant of Muhammad Gorī and afterwards his chief general. He captured Delhi in 1193 and on the death of his master in 1206 took the title of Sulṭān. From that time foreign troops were quartered in

[1] As I have explained in the *Journal of the Royal Asiatic Society*, October, 1926, pp. 717–23, the word *khaṛī*, feminine of *khaṛā*, means standing, and *Khaṛī Bolī* means the standard, current or established language. The word was first used during 1803 by Sadal Miśr in *Nāsiketopākhyān* and by Lallū Lāl in *Prem Sāgar*. *Khaṛī* has nothing to do with *kharī*, pure.

the city. Urdu is always said to have arisen in Delhi, but we must remember that Persian-speaking soldiers entered the Panjab and began to live there, nearly 200 years before the first sultan sat on the throne of Delhi. What is supposed to have happened in Delhi must, in fact, have taken place in Lahore centuries earlier. These troops lived in the Panjab; they doubtless inter-married with the people and within a few years of their arrival must have spoken the language of the country, modified of course by their own Persian mother tongue.

We can picture what happened. The soldiers and people met in daily intercourse and needed a common language It had to be either Persian or Old Panjabi, and the people being in an enormous majority, their language established itself at the expense of the other. For some time the soldiers continued to talk Persian among themselves and the local vernacular with the inhabitants of the country; but ultimately Persian died out, though it continued to be the language of the court, first in Lahore, and later in Delhi, for hundreds of years after it had ceased to be ordinarily spoken in the army. In the Persian which the invaders used there were many Arabic and a few Turkish words; a large number of these were introduced into India.

What happened in Lahore and Delhi resembled in many points what was happening in England after the Norman Conquest. The Normans, speaking a dialect of French, came into an Anglo-Saxon-speaking country and made French the court language. Though they greatly influenced the speech of the conquered country, yet within three centuries they had lost their own language, and England to-day speaks English, blended, it is true, with French. The changes produced in English by the coming of the Normans have probably been exaggerated, but in any case they were greater than those produced in Panjabi and Hindi by the Muslim army. Apart from the incorporation of many loan words the influence was remarkably small. These languages remained practically unchanged in their pronouns, verbs, numerals and grammatical system. The chief change was in vocabulary. In all this English corresponds very closely to Urdu.

Muḥammad Ġorī seized the Panjab in 1187 and his troops under Quṭb ud Dīn Aibak, after consolidating their position, swept on to Delhi, but they cannot have left a hostile Muslim army in the rear. We may be certain that the descendants and successors of the original invaders joined them, and that the two armies marched together to Delhi, which was taken, as we have seen, six years later. When, twelve years later still, the new emperor was installed in Delhi, a large proportion of his soldiers must have spoken by preference a language very like what we think of as early Urdu (the remainder speaking Persian). The basis of that language was Panjabi as it emerged from the Prakrit stage, and it cannot have differed from the Khaṛī of that time nearly as much as the two languages differ to-day. The important fact is that Urdu really began not in Delhi but in Lahore, and that its underlying language was not Khaṛī (much less Braj, as often stated), but old Panjabi. Later on this first form of Urdu was somewhat altered by Khaṛī as spoken round Delhi, but we do not know that Braj exercised any influence at all.

The formation of Urdu began as soon as the Ġaznavī forces settled in Lahore, i.e. in 1027. At what time they gave up Persian and took to speaking Panjabi-Urdu alone, we cannot tell, probably it was a matter of a very few years. One hundred and sixty-six years later the joint Ġorī and Ġaznavī troops entered Delhi. In a short time Urdu was probably their usual language of conversation. We must therefore distinguish two stages: (1) beginning in 1027, Lahore-Urdu, consisting of old Panjabi overlaid by Persian; (2) beginning in 1193, Lahore-Urdu, overlaid by old Khaṛī, not very different then from old Panjabi, and further influenced by Persian, the whole becoming Delhi-Urdu.

When Muhammad Tuġlaq invaded the Deccan and founded Daulatābād (1326), and twenty-one years later when 'Alā ud Dīn Bahmanī rebelled against him and became the first ruler of the Bahmanī dynasty, the Muḥammadan troops who accompanied them spoke Urdu as their mother tongue, and the language which grew up among the Marathi-, Telugu- and Kanarese-speaking inhabitants who became Muslims, was not Persian but Urdu. It is worthy of note that whereas in the north the invaders gave up their own tongue and adopted Urdu, their successors and descendants managed to impose that language, now their own, on a large part of the Deccan, where to-day it is spoken by nearly three million people.

Early History of Urdu. We have no accurate knowledge of spoken Urdu in the early years of its existence. Amīr Khusrau (c. 1255–1325) tells us in his Persian works that he wrote a great deal in 'Hindavi,' but only a little has come down to us; and what we now possess, perhaps 1,000 lines, has doubtless been considerably altered in the passage of time, so that we cannot regard it as correctly showing the speech of his day. We must however emphasize the fact that he did compose literary works in Hindi or Urdu, perhaps both, and that nearly 200 years ago the poet Mīr Taqī accepted as genuine some of the verses which we have to-day. We know this because Mīr refers to them in his anthology.

The word 'Hindi' is used in both a wide and a narrow sense. In the wide sense it includes the languages spoken in Bihār, the United Provinces of Agra and Oudh, Central India, Rājputāna and the S.E. Panjab as far as Ambāla. One might include Kumāon and Gadhvāl. In the narrow sense it means Hindi proper, the chief dialects of which are Braj and Khaṛi. The first writers of Hindi wrote principally in Bihārī, Avadhī, Braj and Rājputānī; languages which were used for both composition and conversation. Muslim authors occasionally employed one of these, but more commonly Persian. Khaṛī, though widespread as a conversational medium, was not much used for literature. Indeed with the exception of Amīr Khusrau's few hundred lines just mentioned, which are mostly in Braj, and the works of the poet Sītal (c. 1723), we have no work in it till we come to the verge of the nineteenth century.

The Urdu branch of Khaṛī has a different history. *Mi'rājul 'Āshiqīn'*, a tract by Banda Navāz, which has recently been printed, and is probably genuine, belongs to the end of the fourteenth century. Seeing that the author left the Deccan when he was fifteen and lived thereafter in Delhi, not returning to the Deccan till he was an old man, we may take his prose as showing the Delhi idiom of that time. In the fifteenth century there is Shāh Mirāṉ Jī of the Deccan, who has left four extant works, and from that time the stream of literature goes on ever widening and deepening.

We must therefore revise our thoughts of both Khaṛī and Urdu. Khaṛī is contemporary with Braj and Avadhī; its beginning may be put at A.D. 900 or 1000. The commencement of Urdu may be dated any time after 1027, when the Muhammadan army of occupation began to live in Lahore. Khaṛī as a spoken language has a continuous history of nearly a thousand years; as a literary language, if we omit Amir Khusrau and one or two other authors, it dates from the end of the eighteenth century. It is difficult to distinguish precisely between Khaṛī and Urdu. For practical purposes the distinction lies in the fact that Khaṛī uses very few, and Urdu very many, Persian and Arabic words. Some people, both Europeans and Indians, have made the use of Hindi or Persian metres the touchstone, but that distinction can be applied only to poetry; it is inapplicable to prose. In poetry, too, some authors, while not varying their language, have employed now Hindi metres, and now Persian. Even at the present day there are poets who sometimes write Urdu poetry in Hindi metres.

There has been a strange reversal of the decrees of fate. The despised Khaṛī language, confined to conversation, and considered unfit for poetry, was not used for serious literary purposes, except by Sital and perhaps Amir Khusrau, till near 1800; so much so that even to-day some persons, not realising that it has had a vigorous existence among the common people since the time when it took the place of Prakrit, think that it was invented by Inshā Allāh, Sadal Miśr and Lallū Lāl. In the Hindi sphere it has now turned out its rivals, and will soon be the only survivor so far as literary work is concerned, while in its Urdu form it has been for centuries the medium of a prosperous and growing literature.

It is important to remember that in the middle of the

fourteenth century there was no real difference between Delhi Urdu and Dakhnī Urdu, but with the establishment of the separate Bahmanī dynasty the two dialects began to diverge.

Urdu literature in its early stages was much more conversational and simple than it was in later years. Probably for that reason it resembles to a surprising degree the spoken language of to-day. This resemblance must not be used as an argument against the genuineness of an early poem or prose work. It shows merely that the author wrote the language as he spoke it. In later years men writing artificially and following foreign models produced works which, divorced from everyday idiom, differ widely from the Urdu which we know now. To take two instances. The Dakhnī poems of Muḥammad Qulī Quṭb Shāh before 1600, and the beautiful Dakhnī poem *Quṭb Mushtarī*, written by Vajhī in 1609, are easier to read than Shāh Naṣīr's writings in the nineteenth century.

The Name 'Urdu.' An important question is how the word 'Urdu' came to be applied to a language. We have seen that the soldiers in Delhi at a very early date gave up the use of Persian among themselves and began to speak a modified form of the vernacular. In Delhi this form of speech, to distinguish it from the usual Khaṛī Bolī (and probably also from Persian), was called *Zabān i Urdū*, the language of the Army, or *Zabān i Urdū e Mu'allā*, the language of the Exalted or Royal Army. As the soldiers and the people intermixed and intermarried, the language spread over the city into the suburbs and even into the surrounding district. It was natural to keep up the separate name to distinguish it not only from the unmixed vernacular of the people, but also from the Persian of the court. This double distinction is not unimportant. It is possible, too, that in time the name served to mark still another distinction, viz. between the speech of Delhi and that of Lucknow. It is supposed that gradually the word 'zabān' was dropped, and 'Urdū' came to be used alone.

In this explanation there is a difficulty. Though the royal camp was established in Delhi during the time of Quṭb ud Dīn Aibak in 1206, the earliest known example of the employment of the word 'Urdū,' standing by itself and meaning the Urdu language, is in the poems of Muṣḥafī, 1750–1824, which are unfortunately undated, and in any case have only in part been printed. Gilchrist uses it in his *Grammar* (1796). The earliest examples of the phrase, *Zabān i Urdū*, the language of the Camp or the Urdu language, are in *Taẕkira e Gulzār i Ibrāhīm* by 'Alī Ibrahīm Khān (1783) and in Muṣḥafī's *Taẕkira e Shu'arā e Hindī* (1794). In this title we must note the word 'Hindī' (meaning 'Urdū'). The expression *Zabān i Urdū e mu'allā (e Shāhjahānābād Dihlī)*, the language of the Royal Camp, or the Exalted Urdu language (of Shāhjahānābād, Delhi) occurs in the anthology *Nikāt ush Shu'arā* by Mīr Taqī (1752). In Qiyām ud Dīn Qāim's anthology *Makhzan i Nikāt* (1754) we find *muḥāvira e Urdū e mu'allā*, the idiom of the Royal Camp. 'Arsh, the son of Mīr Taqī, speaks of himself as *Urdū e mu'allā kā zabāndān*, one well acquainted with the Urdū e Mu'allā language. His date is unknown, but he seems to have been born in Mīr's old age.

Now the earliest of these is five and a half centuries after the foreign army had settled in Delhi; and we naturally ask why during all this long period the language never received the name 'Urdu,' and why people suddenly thought of that name after the lapse of so long a time, when it had ceased to have any particular meaning. This period of 550 years could perhaps be reduced; it has been claimed, but not proved, that the royal camp in Delhi was not known as the Urdu till the time of Bābur, who came direct from Turkistan with a Turki force in 1526. It is a doubtful point. We may admit that before his time the foreign recruits had nearly all been Persian speakers or descendants of Persian speakers. But on the other hand the word 'Urdū' for army had been in Persian since 1150, for it is found more than once in the *Jahāṅkushā* of Javainī with that meaning.

The first example of it in India is said to be in the *Tuzuk i Bāburī*, compiled by the Emperor Bābur himself in 1529. But even if we accept these later dates for the first occurrence in India of the word 'Urdū' with the meaning of army, we still have to account for the fact that for

226 years, from 1526 to 1752 no one seems to have thought of calling the language by that name, and that it was only after 1752 that this was done. It is almost incredible that none of the historians of the Mugal period ever used the name; yet such seems to have been the case. The language as spoken was generally called Hindi; when employed for literary, that is poetical, purposes it was known as Rekhta (see p. 3) or Hindi. Amīr Khusrau and Shekh Bājan (d. 1506) speak of *Zabān i Dihlavī*, the speech of Delhi; while Vajhī in *Sab Ras* (1634) calls it *Zabān i Hindostān*, the language of Hindustan. But no one in the early days spoke of 'Urdu.' Even in the end of the eighteenth century it was an uncommon word. People continued to talk of Hindi and Rekhta. As late as 1790 'Abd ul Qādir in the preface to his Urdu translation of the Qur'ān said he was translating not into Rekhta but into Hindī.

One interesting detail is still *sub judice*. It has been asserted that the Persian dictionary, *Mu'ayyid ul Fuzalā* (1519) uses the phrase, 'in the language of the people of the Urdu.' But it is claimed on the other hand that the words are not found in good MSS. of the Dictionary; and the MS. in the British Museum does not appear to contain them. Even if it did, 'urdu' would not here be the name of a language. It is a fact worth noting that the word 'Urdū' is not given in this Dictionary at all with any meaning, either 'army' or any other. Possibly the explanation of the problem is that *Zabān i Urdū*, the speech of the Camp, or some equivalent phrase, was in conversational use from the earliest times, and that gradually, centuries later, it was admitted to books, while the use of the word 'Urdu' alone, without *zabān*, was still later. But the subject requires further investigation.

The Place of Urdu among Languages. The great Indo-European family of languages is divided into Italic, Teutonic, Keltic, Greek, Albanian, Slavonic, Armenian and Aryan sub-families. The Aryan sub-family has two main branches, Iranian and Indo-Aryan or Sanskritic. (The Kāfir languages may belong to the latter, but probably should be classed by themselves as a third branch.) During the course of the second millennium B.C. the Aryans came from Central Asia into India. The Mauryan Dynasty was established before 320 B.C., and Ashoka, 250 B.C., ruled over a settled empire extending from Calcutta to beyond Kābul. At that time Sanskrit was spoken over the whole of north India; there were different dialects, but all were closely connected with Vedic Sanskrit. It is remarkable that there is practically nothing in the phonology of the modern Aryan languages of India which cannot be directly derived from an early form of Sanskrit, essentially the same as that of the Vedas.

There are to-day, if we exclude the Kāfir group, approximately 23 to 26 languages descended from Sanskrit. In the case of some, we can trace the intermediate stages fairly well; in the case of others, we possess nothing between Sanskrit and the modern language. The following is a fairly complete list of the Indo-Aryan languages:

Sindhī
Lahndī
Panjābī
Hindī
Gujrātī (with Bhīlī)
Rājputānī (with Khāndeshī)
Pahāṛī languages:
  Kumāonī
  Gaḍhwālī (Central Pahāṛī)
  Western Pahāṛī
  Nepālī
Avadhī or Pūrabī (Eastern Hindī)

Bihārī
Uṛiyā
Bengālī (with Assamese)
Marāṭhī
Singhalese
Dard languages:
  Ṣinā
  Kashmīrī
  Kohistānī
Five allied languages:
  Chitrālī, Tīrāhī, Pashai, Kalāshā and Gavarbaṭī

Of these, Hindī, which immediately concerns us, has two important dialects, Braj and Khaṛī Bolī; Khaṛī Bolī again has three forms, (1) Urdu, which contains many Persian and Arabic words; (2) Literary Hindī, which has many Sanskrit words; and (3) Hindustānī, a commonsense *via media* between the other two, hardly to be distinguished from simple Urdu. Finally, spoken Urdu has two varieties: (i) Daknī or Dakhnī, spoken in the Deccan, and (ii) Northern Urdu spoken in north India.

II

THE BEGINNINGS OF URDU LITERATURE

THIS chapter deals with the first 380 years of Urdu literature. We may divide the time into two parts: first, the Religious period, 1350–1590, during which poems and tracts were written simply to teach the elements of religion; and second, the Literary period, 1590–1730, during which the writing of Urdu was practically confined to the Deccan, while Muslim writers in the north wrote Persian.

It is an astonishing fact that literary composition in Urdu was going on in the Deccan for hundreds of years before it really began in north India. In order to understand this, we must remind ourselves of the history of the country. An early form of Urdu was introduced into the Deccan by the soldiers of 'Alā ud Dīn Khilji who became Sultan in 1296. Between 1294 and 1311 there were many raids upon the Deccan conducted chiefly by his favourite, Malik Kāfūr, but the country was only partially subdued. In 1326, however, the Emperor Muḥammad Ṭuglaq forsook Delhi and founded Daulatābād in the Deccan, close to where Aurangābād now stands; 21 years later, while he was occupied elsewhere, his officer, Ẓafar Khān, declared his independence, took the name of 'Alā ud Dīn and became the first ruler of the Bahmani dynasty of the Deccan, which remained in power till 1500, and lasted without power for 18 years longer. The capital was Gulbarga.

At this stage there are two points to be kept in mind. First, the new king had just revolted against the Emperor of Delhi. Consequently he and his people wished to be as separate as possible from the capital; they developed a local patriotism with a desire to emphasise their own life and modes of thought; and lastly they began to suspect and dislike outsiders. This resulted in a cultivation of Urdu, as opposed to Persian which was the language of the Emperor's court. Their Urdu was influenced of course by local vernaculars, especially Gujrātī and Marhaṭī (Marāṭhī), and was called not Urdu, but Dakhni or Dakni. Most of the writers mentioned in this chapter used that dialect, and the word 'Urdu,' when referring to them, is used in that sense. The invading Musalmans and their descendants spoke it, the Muslim converts and their descendants did the same; soon it became the language of the court itself, though Persian remained the language of the Delhi court for centuries after this. It must be remembered that down to about 1375 there was little difference between Dakhni Urdu and Delhi Urdu.

The second point is that the desire to spread the doctrines of Islam necessitated the use of the vernacular for the purposes of propaganda; and so many religious terms were introduced into the language, for the holy men who have always played an important part in the life of the Deccan, began to write tracts and even larger works in Dakhni. We have already seen that the earliest writings were religious, and that some of them were written nearly 400 years before there was any regular Urdu composition in Delhi.

The linguistic importance of the Religious period is very great, for here we see the language in its earliest known form. There was no attempt at literary finish; men wrote as they felt led with a view to imparting spiritual instruction. Most of the writers were well-known teachers. Much of their work has been lost, but what survive includes both poetry and prose; most of it is in Dakhni. The following is a summary:

Thirteenth century—*Shekh Shakar Ganj* (see No. 11).

Fourteenth century—*Shāh Banda Nawāz*; the unknown author of *Haft Asrār*; *'Abdullāh Husainī*.

Fifteenth century—*Mīrān Jī and Shekh Bājan*.

Sixteenth century—*Shāh Burhān*; *Shāh 'Alī Jyū*; *Khūb Muhammad*; and the author of *Nūr Nāma*.

During the reign of the last Bahmani king, Mahmūd

Shāh (1482–1518), the provincial viceroys broke away and established five separate kingdoms, the dynasty coming to an end in 1518. Of these states by far the most important from the literary point of view were Golkuṇḍa and Bījāpūr.

The Literary period began near the end of the sixteenth century. At that time the Deccan was still divided into five kingdoms. In two of them the kings were themselves eager patrons of literature, both Persian and Urdu. There were therefore two centres of poetry, Golkuṇḍa (or after 1589, Ḥaidarābād), the seat of the Quṭb Shāhī dynasty, 1518–1687, and Bījāpūr, the seat of the ʿĀdil Shāhī dynasty, 1490–1686, which was generally Shīʿa in belief. This condition of affairs lasted for about a hundred years, till 1687 in Ḥaidarābād and 1686 in Bījāpūr, when the local rulers were deposed by the Emperor Aurangzeb. Anarchy prevailed till his death in 1707, but did not entirely put a stop to the pursuit of letters.

A. THE RELIGIOUS PERIOD, A.D. 1350–1590

It has been asserted that prose was written as early as 1100, but nothing is known about it and the statement is almost certainly incorrect.

1. Shekh ʿAin ud Dīn, Ganj ul ʿIlm (1306–93), born in Delhi, came to Daulatābād in the time of Muḥammad Tuglaq (1325–51) and died in Bījāpūr. He wrote chiefly in Persian but is believed to have been the author of some Dakhnī tracts on the duties of religion.

2. Khāja Banda Navāz, Gīsū Darāz (said to have been born in 1321, d. 1422) wrote two short prose works, *Miʿrāj ul ʿĀshiqīn*, which has recently been printed, and *Hidāyat Nāma*, both religious. The former is of great importance as being the earliest printed example of Urdu prose. It is a Ṣūfī tract, nineteen pages long.

3. A pupil of Banda Navāz wrote a large commentary on his master's sayings, and called it *Haft Asrār*.

4. ʿAbdullāh Ḥusainī, a grandson of Banda Navāz, translated ʿAbdul Qādir Jīlānī's Arabic tract, *Nishāṭ ul ʿIshq*, and wrote a commentary on it. This work and *Haft Asrār* may be dated near the end of the fourteenth century.

5. SHĀH MĪRĀN JĪ, SHAMS UL 'USHSHĀQ (d. 1496), one of the Bījāpūr saints, preached and wrote in Urdu. He is the author of two interesting poems which have for their heroine a very religious, but perhaps imaginary, girl of seventeen, called Khush or Khushnūdī, who renounces the world and devotes herself to obtaining spiritual teaching from Mīrāṉ Jī. The first, 350 lines long, is called *Khush Nāma*, and the second, which continues the story, the girl asking questions and Mīrāṉ Jī replying, is named *Khush Naghz*. It is 146 lines in length. The author's name occurs four times in *Khush Nāma*.

More important, but less charming, is *Shahādat ul Haqīqat*, a poem of 1,126 lines, notable for a striking passage in which the author tells why he preached and wrote in Urdu, the language which all would understand. A short prose work, *Sharḥ i Marghūb ul Qulūb*, is with good reason attributed to him. Its importance is linguistic. It is the earliest Urdu prose we have except Banda Navāz's *Mi'rāj ul 'Āshiqīn*. He is said also to have written *Jal Tarang* and *Gul Bās*, both in prose.

6. SHĀH BURHĀN (d. 1582) was the son of Mīrāṉ Jī (No. 5). He wrote a considerable quantity of both verse and prose, in what he called Hindī or Gujarī, meaning by the latter term Dakhnī tinged with Gujrātī words and phrases. Ten of his religious poems are extant; most of them are short, but one, *Hujjat ul Baqā*, extends to 1,610 lines, and one, called *Irshād Nāma*, is 5,000 lines long. In this poem he gives, as his father had done in *Shahādat ul Haqīqat*, his reasons for writing Urdu instead of Persian. Most of his metres are Hindī, and his language is full of Hindī expressions; but it is Urdu, not Hindī. The writers we have considered were religious men, expressing Ṣūfī ideas, and writing to instruct their followers; yet in Shāh Burhān's poems there is not a little true poetry. He produced also several prose works, one of which, *Kalimat ul Haqāiq*, is of considerable length.

In this section we may include the following:

7. SHĀH MĪRĀN JĪ KHUDĀNUMĀ (d. 1659), at one time servant of King 'Abdullāh Quṭb Shāh, was consecrated successor to Amīn ud Dīn A'lā (No. 8), but died before his

master. He wrote in 1600 a prose work called *Sharḥ i Sharḥ i Tamhīd*, a translation of, or commentary on, a Persian religious work. It is important as one of the earliest examples of Urdu prose. The style is plain, simple and straightforward. One extant MS. of it was written in 1603.

8. Amīn ud Dīn A'lā (1582–1675), the son of Shāh Burhān (No. 6), was a religious teacher, who, in addition to an ode on his father, wrote *Muḥibb Nāma*, or *Muḥabbat Nāma*, an ode on spiritual love, and *Rumūz us Sālikīn*, a poem on the unity of God and other subjects. He wrote also a religious poem without a name, some verses in Hindi *dohrā* metre, and some mixed Persian and Hindi lines. Of his prose tracts the most important are *Guftār i Ḥaẓrat Shāh Amīn* and *Ganj i Makhfī*. His writings have a religious rather than a literary value. He is sometimes credited with a large number of short poetical romances, collected in MS. called *Javāhir ul Asrār*, and with two poems, *Risāla e Qurbīya* and *Risāla e Vujūdīya* which have 640 lines between them.

9. *Miftāḥ ul Khairāt*, an anonymous prose work (probably about 1630), is an exposition of religious duties.

10. In 1662, 'Abdullāh wrote *Aḥkām uṣ Salavāt*, a prose translation from Persian. It gives rules for prayer and contains a compendium of Ḥanafī tenets. This work has been printed as part of Shāh Malik's *Sharī'at Nāma* (No. 51).

During this period there were a few Urdu religious writers in other parts of India, especially the Panjab and Gujrat. (Such are Nos. 11–19 below.)

11. Shekh Farīd ud Dīn, Shakar Ganj (d.1266), was born near Multān and died in Pāk Paṭan. A few lines of doubtful authenticity are extant which show a mixture of Urdu, Panjabi and Persian.

12. Shekh Bahā ud Dīn Bājan (d. 1506) was a religious teacher, a little of whose writing has come down to us. It is in mixed Hindi and Urdu.

13. Shāh 'Alī Jyū of Aḥmadābād, Gujrat (d. 1565), whose full name was Shāh 'Alī Muḥammad Jyū Gām Dhanī, wrote a religious poem called *Javāhir ul Asrār Allāh*, generally known as his *Dīvān*. The poem, about

4,800 lines in length, tells of the poet's love for God. The style is simple and attractive, and the language shows strong Gujrati influence.

14. SHEKH KHŪB MUHAMMAD, also of Ahmadābād, was a disciple of Shekh Kamāl Muhammad whose teachings he set forth in *Khūb Tarang* (1578), a poem of much linguistic importance. The India Office copy is only 29 years later.

15. NŪR NĀMA is an anonymous religious poem of about the same time as *Khūb Tarang*. It shows Panjabi influence.

16. SHEKH 'USMĀN (1625). 17. SHEKH JUNAID (c. 1650). 18. VALĪ RĀM. All from the Panjab; wrote Persian verse with a few lines of Urdu scattered through it.

19. 'ABDĪ, 1663, is the author of *Fiqh i Hindī*, wrongly attributed by Sprenger to Shekh Jīvan. It is in Urdu but with many Panjabi expressions.

B. THE FIRST LITERARY PERIOD OF URDU IN THE DECCAN, 1590–1730

It is convenient to divide this period into three parts, the first two running parallel: (1) Literature in Golkunda or Haidarābād, connected with the Qutb Shāhī court (1590–1687); (2) Literature in Bījāpūr, connected with the 'Ādil Shāhī Court (1590–1686); (3) Literature in the Deccan during the time of Aurangzeb and his successors (1687–1730).

The greatest poets of this period were the following:

GOLKUNDA: Muhammad Qulī Qutb Shāh, King of Golkunda (1580–1611); Vajhī (flor. 1600–40); Gavvāsī (1639); Ibn i Nishātī (1655); Tab'ī (1670).

BIJĀPŪR: Rustamī (1649); Nusratī (1650–70); Mirzā (1660).

1687–1730: Valī and Sirāj, both of Aurangābād.

The greatest of these was Valī.

The Quṭb Shāhī Poets

20. **Muhammad Quli Qutb Shah.**[1] Muḥammad Qulī Quṭb Shāh, the fourth king of the Quṭb Shāhi dynasty, reigned in Golkuṇḍa from 1580 to 1611. Nine years after he came to the throne he founded the city of Ḥaidarābād and made it his capital. Scholars and religious leaders flocked to his court. The king led the way in learning and poetry; he was a prolific writer in both Persian and Dakhnī. His works were collected shortly after his death by his nephew and successor, Muḥammad Quṭb Shāh. A beautiful copy, consisting of nearly 1,800 pages with about 100,000 lines, was made in 1616, only five years after the author's death, and still exists.

This royal poet is possibly, even probably, the first literary writer of Urdu. Previous writers had written for the purpose of instruction; but his works are purely literary. He deals with a great variety of subjects; indeed breadth of mind and width of interest are his most notable characteristics. He was the first Urdu author to write odes, lyrics, romances and real elegies. His religious poems are numerous and good, though conventional. His love poems are truly Indian in style, not Persian. In addition to the usual subjects beloved of Persian poets and their Urdu followers, he entered into matters of everyday life, describing Hindu and Muhammadan feasts and festivals, celebrations of birthdays and marriages, the customs prevailing in the country, life in his own royal palace, even fruits and vegetables, birds and flowers—in short, he might have said with Terence, *humani nihil a me alienum puto.* The only later Urdu poets who compare with him in this respect are Saudā and Naẓīr; they are inferior to him in description of nature, while he is superior to Naẓīr in his sympathetic account of Hindu life, which Saudā did not touch. It is astonishing that the first poet should have been so well-equipped.

[1] The names of the more important writers in the pages which follow are printed in heavier type than the others; e.g. Nos. 20, 24, etc.

Poems by Muḥammad Quli Quṭb Shāh

I. THE LITTLE DARK GIRL

1. Mine eyes have seen a little girl's dark face
   and have become forgetful of all else.
2. Thy cypress form comes out coquettishly
   and lights appear to me like moon-rays fair.
3. Swift as the wind her hands surround her waist,
   that golden waist then shines like sun and moon.
4. No wonder that her radiance conquers me,
   the light of earth and heaven : who knows it not ?
5. Thy absence drear affrights me from afar ;
   how can she know her home is in my heart ?

II. MY BIRTHDAY

1. Through the prayer of the Prophet I've now reached my birthday
   And beaten the drums sounding forth the good news.
2. I have drunk at the hand of Muḥammad sweet nectar ;
   God therefore has made me the crown over kings.
3. The Pole Star, my name star, is nobler than all,
   My canopy coloured expands in the sky.
4. The sun and the moon both are clashing like cymbals
   With sky for arena and tambourines' sound.
5. There Jupiter dances to honour my birthday,
   While Venus is chanting a victory song.
6. My garden is thus overflowing with freshness,
   And furnishes fruit every hour of the day.
7. My enemies all in one place God has gathered
   And wishes to burn them like incense in fire.
8. Fulfil, O my God, all my hope's expectation,
   As Thou gladdenest the earth with the soft rain of peace.
9. The favour of God has brought me my birthday,
   Give true thanks to Him for thy birthday now reached.
10. Through prayers of the priests my kingdom stands firmly,
    God gives me to drink of the water of life.

III. LIFE IN A LOVE

1. Without the loved one wine cannot be drunk,
   Nor without her one moment life be lived.
2. They said : ' Show patience absent from your love ' ;
   This can be said, but surely not be done.
3. The man who knows not love is merciless,
   Never with such a one hold speech or sit.
4. I am distracted, give me no advice,
   Never to such as I is counsel given.

21. Fīroz, a poet whose works are not extant. Vajhi in the prologue to *Quṭb Mushtarī* says he was a great poet and an authority on Urdu poetry. Ibn i Nishāṭī called him a 'master.'

22. Sayyid Maḥmūd, too, is known to us only through his being mentioned by Vajhi and Ibn i Nishāṭī, the latter of whom refers to his good poetical taste.

23. Aḥmad Daknī, a poet at the court of Quli Quṭb Shāh, is said to have written in 1600 a romance called *Lailā-Majnūn* of which 2,000 lines are extant. Nothing is known about him, but he is favourably mentioned by Ibn i Nishāṭī.

24. **Vajhi.** Vajhī is the author of *Quṭb Mushtarī* (1609), a poem referred to as anonymous and nameless on p. 64 of the India Office Catalogue. It is a romantic fairy story relating the adventures of the prince who afterwards became King of Golkuṇḍa. (See No. 20 above.) He dreamt of an unknown princess, fell in love with her and set out in search of her. Finally he found her and married her. This remarkable poem is thoroughly Indian. The Urdu is good, the description bright, varied and natural. His thoughts and language are original, and he must rank as one of the truest and greatest poets in Urdu. It contains a number of simple lyrics.

In 1634 he wrote an important prose religious story called *Sab Ras*, modelled as regards style upon Ẓuhūrī's Persian preface to *Nauras Nāma* (No. 43); the prose is both rhythmical and rhymed; yet it is simple and flowing. It is probably a translation of a Persian work by Vajih ud Din Gujrātī. Ṣūfī teachings are presented in narrative form. It is the first literary prose in the language. The story runs right through, but is spoilt by constant sermonising. All the characters have allegorical names such as Beauty, Heart, Love and Faithfulness. Vajhī was Poet Laureate during the reign of Qulī Quṭb Shāh, and in the prologue to his poem he satirised his contemporaries, especially G̱avvāṣī; but 30 years later when he wrote *Sab Ras* times had changed. 'Abdullāh Quṭb Shāh was then king and G̱avvāṣī was the favourite poet.

Poems from Vajhī's "Qutb Mushtari"

I. THE DAWN OF LOVE

1. Not on earth she appeared nor in heaven.
   The prince recked of naught but the maid;
2. He was restless in numberless ways.
   Nor in words could the matter be told,
3. Nor yet could all understand,
   Only he upon whom it had passed.
4. In this state he remained night and day,
   With himself alone had he speech.
5. The charmer absorbed all his thought,
   Like amber attracting the grass.
6. He arose, but anon went and slept,
   For the maid was seen only in dreams.
7. If the friend comes thus in a dream,
   Then the lover wants nothing but sleep.
8. Bewildered, distressed and perturbed—
   No peace all the day, save in sleep.
9. Not openly can it be told,
   To whom can I trust this my woe?
10. On my couch I'm a tossing sea surge,
    For my dream friend my thirst has aroused.

II. A WINE FEAST

1. One night the Emperor an assembly made;
   The sons of ministers sat with him there,
2. And every youth was handsome, fair to see,
   And winsome every one with youthful charm;
3. In war as unafraid as great King Jam,
   In bravery not Rustam's self more brave.
4. Courtiers and singers, elegant and wise,
   Sat in one place together with the King.
5. Goblet and pitcher taking in their hand
   The courtiers one and all engaged in talk;
6. And when the singers rhythmically sang,
   The earth was trembling with the jovial sound.
7. Upon them, as they sang in that wild waste,
   A frenzy passed through overmuch desire;
8. And they that served the King in minstrelsy
   Were adding melody to melody.
9. The singers entering into merriment
   Would presently make even mourners gay.
10. With wine and pitcher, salted fruits and cup,
    Intoxicated all the guests became.
11. When half the night was come and midnight lowered
    Bereft of sense were friends with sense before.
12. Courtiers remembered not how to converse
    And singers their surroundings heeded not.

25. **Gavvasi.** G̲avvāṣī was in later life attached to the court. He is the author of two works. The first is a romance called *Qiṣṣa e Saif ul Mulūk o Badī' ul Jamāl*, 14,000 lines long, which tells of the love of the Egyptian prince, Saif ul Mulūk, for a Chinese princess; it is a Dakhnī version of a story in the Persian *Arabian Nights*. Different MS. copies give the date as 1616, 1618 and 1624. This is a great favourite and has been translated into several Indian languages. From the preface we learn that the author was very poor; he was also very conceited and thought little of the merits of other poets. When he wrote his second work, nearly 20 years later, he was evidently popular and well off. He was a good poet, but not equal to his contemporaries, Vajhī and Ibn i Nishāṭī. He wrote much better in the days of his poverty than he did afterwards when fortune smiled upon him. His other poem is a romance, *Ṭūṭī Nāma*, the tales of a parrot, a poetical translation of Ẓiyā ud Dīn's Persian work of the same name, which is itself based upon a Sanskrit original. It was written in 1639. Before beginning the poem proper the poet writes a long ode in praise of his master 'Abdullāh Quṭb Shāh.

26. Muḥammad Quṭb Shāh, Ẓill Ullāh, reigned in Ḥaidarābād (1611–24). He collected his predecessor's poetry and wrote a poetical preface. In an extant MS. of his works there are many notes in his own handwriting giving useful information about other poets and their writings. He was more learned than his uncle, but his poetry, though not without charm, is a good deal inferior.

27. 'Abdullāh Quṭb Shāh was King of Ḥaidarābād (1624–72). His poems, along with those of the poet just mentioned (No. 26), were collected in 1667. The MS. is in Ḥaidarābād, but has not been printed. During his long reign, Urdu poetry flourished in Ḥaidarābād. We are well informed about it because we have the contemporary history, *Hadīqat us Salāṭīn*, by his own historian Niẓām ud Dīn Aḥmad.

28. Quṭbī was the author of *Tuḥfat un Naṣāiḥ* (1637), an unimportant poem containing over 1,500 lines; it is a translation of a Persian religious work by Shekh Yūsuf of Delhi. The metre and rhyme are the same as in the

Persian, and the translation follows the original line by line. Quṭbī lived in Ḥaidarābād, and must be distinguished from the Quṭbī who wrote *Terah Māsā* over a hundred years later. The second Quṭbī was a disciple of Jān Jānāṉ Maẓhar.

29. MUQĪMĪ is a poet of whom next to nothing is known. In a mediocre original poem which has come down to us he mentions his being a friend of Ġavvāṣī (No. 25) which suggests that he too belonged to Ḥaidarābād. He wrote a romance called *Qiṣṣa e Candarbadan o Mahyār*. Candarbadan is a Hindu princess who refuses an offer of marriage from a Muhammadan named Mahyār, but on his death from a broken heart renounces her religion and dies. They are buried together. The story resembles that of Mīr's *Shuʿla e ʿIshq* (No. 104).

30. ʿALĪ AKBAR AḤMAD JUNAIDĪ of the Quṭb Shāhī court lived in the time of ʿAbdullāh Quṭb Shāh (1624–72), and composed in 1654 a romance entitled *Māh Paikar*.

31. **Ibn i Nishati.** IBN I NISHĀṬĪ wrote in 1655 *Phūlban*, a romance, 3,500 lines in length. From both the literary and the historical standpoint it is of great value. Although in the main it is a translation of a Persian work, *Basātīn*, written during the reign of Muhammad Tuġlaq in the early part of the fourteenth century by Aḥmad Zubairī, it is a living picture of the life of the beginning of the seventeenth century. Like other romances of the time it begins with praise to God and the saints; after exalting the virtues of the king it goes on to tell of social festivities. When the story is completed the author laments the death of some of his poet predecessors. In the epilogue, written years later and historically valuable, he tells us that he had written prose (none of it is extant now), but says that this is his first attempt at poetry. We learn that his poem brought him much popularity. The illustrated MS. in the India Office was prepared at the order of a well-to-do lady in Sidhoṭ. There appears to be no ground for saying that he wrote a *Ṭūṭī Nāma* or that he ever used the name, ʿAvarī.' He had quite a modest estimate of his own ability. *Phūlban* is superior to Nuṣratī's work (see No. 49) in the simplicity and fluency of its language, but inferior in thought and narrative.

It is one of the best romances of the Quṭb Shāhī age. Some say that the author was a Shīʻa.

32. Mīrān Ya'qūb in 1668, or a little later, translated *Shamāil ul Atqiā*, a long work by Khāja Burhān ud Dīn of Aurangābād. The style is simple and attractive.

33. **Tab'ī.** Ṭab'ī of Golkunda, who lived during the reigns of the last two kings of Ḥaidarābād, wrote a fine romance called *Qiṣṣa e Bahrām o Gul Andām*. It was written in 1670; the preface was dedicated to Shāh Rājū, a contemporary saint. The romance is based upon Niẓāmī's *Haft Paikar*; it was written in forty days. Ṭab'ī had a great reverence for Vajhī who appeared to him in a dream and praised his work. He regarded Vajhī as his poetical master and followed him. His poem shows much originality and is of higher merit than the two versions of the theme produced by Amīn and Daulat, known as *Bahrām o Bānu Ḥusn*. (Nos. 45, 46.) Ṭab'ī's poem, which is nearly 2,700 lines long, is divided into sections of equal length. It contains an excellent ode on Khāja Banda Navāz (No. 2).

34. Abu'l Ḥasan Tānā Shāh was King of Ḥaidarābād from 1672 down to 1687 when Aurangzeb dethroned and imprisoned him. It is certain that he was a poet like the three kings before him, but his work is not extant. It was probably destroyed during his imprisonment; only a few lines are now known.

35, 36. Nūrī. Two men of this name are sometimes confused. One, a friend of Faiẓī in the time of Akbar, occasionally wrote half couplets in Urdu; the other, No. 36, who was a courtier of the king just mentioned, was probably the Nūrī known to have been a famous elegy-writer. Some say that the earlier Nūrī also wrote elegies and that in later life he made Bījāpūr his home.

37. Muḥammad Amīn wrote an unfinished poem, 1,200 lines long, called *Qiṣṣa e Abu Shaḥma*, a story about the son of the Khalifa 'Umr bin Khaṭṭāb. The author was a mere boy at the time. He lived apperently in or near Ḥaidarābād under 'Abdullāh Quṭb Shāh. (No. 27.)

38. Abu'l Qāsim Mirzā was a servant of Tānā Shāh. After his patron was taken captive and dethroned by

Aurangzeb in 1687 Mirzā retired to ʿAbdullāh Ganj near the capital, lived there as a *darvesh*, and there died. His poems are not extant. He is the author of a romance, *Jang Nāma* (doubtful), translated from Persian, and of an elegy, in which he relates the story of the fighting of Ḥanif, the son of ʿAlī, with Yazīd and his followers.

39. Shāh Qulī Khān Shāhī, a native of Bhavnagar, was a good elegy writer who lived in Ḥaidarābād in the time of Tānā Shāh. One short elegy is particularly good. He wrote also odes and lyrics. We may put his date at 1680. He was a court poet and everyone was fond of him.

40. Fāiz belonged to Golkunda. In 1683 he wrote a romance, 1,700 lines long, called *Rizvān Shāh o Rūḥ Afzā*, in which he told the story of the love of Rizvān Shāh, prince of China, for Rūḥ Afzā, a Jinn princess. Like many other works of the time it is a translation from Persian. He was a very modest man and wrote not for gain or reward, but because he felt compelled to do so. The British Museum MS. has a pathetic interest. It belonged to Major M. W. Carr, Madras Staff Corps, who was about to edit it when he was drowned (January 13, 1871). Fāiz used many Arabic and Persian words and constructions. In this he resembled Vali (No. 75) rather than earlier Dakhni writers. We are thus enabled to put a date to the beginning of the Persianising tendency.

41. Shuʿūr (c. 1680) was another poet of the time of Tānā Shāh.

42. Laṭīf in 1684 wrote a long poem of little merit, called *Ẓafar Nāma*, about as long as *Paradise Lost*. It describes the wars of Ḥanif. Its interest is religious.

The ʿĀdil Shāhī Poets

43. Another royal poet was Ibrāhīm ʿĀdil Shāh II, King of Bījāpūr (1580–1626), who in 1599 founded near his capital a garden city, giving it the name of Naurasрūr. This was intended to be a great religious and literary centre. Shortly afterwards the king wrote a poem on music called *Nauras Nāma*, to which the Persian writer, Ẓuhūrī, wrote a preface. The poem was in Dakhnī, and Hindi metres

were employed throughout. In this king's reign many poets and scholars came from Gujrat.

44. Ātishī, a Persian poet (flor. 1620) wrote some Urdu poetry, not now extant, but popular in its day.

45. Amīn was the author of an incomplete romance, *Bahrām o Bānū Ḥusn* (about 1620), which was finished in 1639 by Daulat Shāh (No. 46). It tells in smooth and easy language the exploits of Bahrām Gor, the Persian king, while in the land of the Jinns, and of his marrying Bānū Ḥusn, the daughter of the king of the country. The story is much liked and has been told several times.

46. Daulat Shāh, a Persian poet who latterly wrote in Urdu. As has just been mentioned he completed Amīn's poem in 1639.

47. Malik Khushnūd lived in the time of Muḥammad 'Ādil Shāh, whose Poet Laureate he was. He wrote two romances in a crabbed and awkward style. One, named *Bahrām*, containing 6,500 lines, is in the style of Khusrau's *Hasht Bihisht*. The British Museum Catalogue wrongly calls the author Muḥammad Shāh. The other, *Yūsuf-Zulekhā*, is also adapted from Khusrau. In 1635 he was sent as an ambassador to Golkunda.

48. **Rustumi.** Kamāl Khān Rustumī was the son of Khaṭṭāt Khān, secretary to the royal court of Bījāpūr. In 1649 he completed a long romance called *Khāvar Nāma*, more than twice as long as *The Ring and the Book*. It relates the story of 'Alī, and was written at the request of the princess Khadīja, a person of great importance in the literary world of the time. She was the sister of 'Abdullāh Quṭb Shāh (No. 27) and wife of Muḥammad 'Ādil Shāh, who was King of Bījāpūr (1626–56). This poet is called Rustumi by Ethé and Blumhardt, and Rasmi by Garcin de Tassy. On metrical grounds the latter name must be wrong. His work has considerable value, for it is the first epic in Urdu, and north India has no Urdu epic poetry, apart from elegies. The poem, which is a version of a Persian work is in simple and flowing language. He was also a good prose-writer.

49. **Nusrati.** Nuṣratī was a poet who flourished in the court of 'Alī 'Ādil Shāh (1656–73). He wrote three romances. *Gulshan i 'Ishq* (1657), 8,000 lines long, resembles Khush-

nūd's *Bahrām* fifteen or twenty years earlier. It does not rank high as poetry. He was urged to write it because of the paucity of Dakhnī romances on the Persian model. It describes the mutual love of Prince Manohar and Madhumālati. *'Alī Nāma*, composed some years later, is a long account of the glorious deeds of his royal master. It is superior to every other poem produced in Bijāpūr. It tells the history of 'Alī 'Ādil Shah's reign for ten years, (1656–66) and is the first biography in the language. Scattered through it are fine odes, mostly on military subjects, which place the author's name high among Urdu ode writers. He writes powerfully with more description and less panegyric than the poets of north India. An earlier work, *Mi'rāj Nāma*, written during the reign of Muhammad 'Ādil Shāh, contains many more Dakhnī expressions than the others and is more difficult to understand. Some of his critics objected to the local words employed in it; but he replied, 'A customer is concerned with getting a good bargain, not with the ceiling and roof of the shop.' It is said that his *'Alī Nāma* was composed to show that he could, when he liked, write in another style. He left also a collection of odes, and one of lyrics known as *Guldasta e 'Ishq*. Nuṣratī excelled in power of imagination, freshness of subjects, and in the fitness of his words to express his thoughts; he was good at impromptu composition and in humorous verses. He died at an advanced age in the year 1683. His *'Alī Nāma* is his best work and it is very important. Upon it he expended his full strength and through it he conferred immortality upon his hero, the king.

50. **Mirza.** MIRZĀ (1660) lived in the time of 'Alī 'Ādil Shāh (1656–73) and wrote some good elegies. He never wrote encomiums on kings or nobles, but he is the author of verses in honour of Muḥammadan saints.

51. SHĀH MALIK wrote in 1666 *Sharī 'at Nāma*, a religious poem, 508 lines long, containing details of observances incumbent upon pious Muslims. It includes *Aḥkām us Salāt* also found as a separate MS. The style is simple.

52. SEVĀ of Gulbarga, who lived in Bijāpūr, wrote or translated in 1680 a collection of elegies with the title

Rauẓat ush Shuhadā. He set an example to other Dakhnī poets, and translations of this work became fashionable. He wrote also *Qānūn i Islām* in which rules for prayer are given.

53. 'Abd ul Mūmin Mūmin lived in Mysore but was connected with Bījāpūr. In 1681 he wrote a large book, *Asrār i 'Ishq*, a copy of which still exists. In this he related the life and miracles of Sayyid Muḥammad Jaunpūrī.

54. Mīrān Hāshimī (d. 1697) was the spiritual disciple of Shāh Hāshim from whom he derived his second name. In 1687 he composed a long romance of 12,000 lines called *Yūsuf-Zulekhā*. On the strength of the speeches attributed to Zulekhā he has been called the first writer of rekhtī (pp. 42, 54), but this is not correct, for when a woman is represented as speaking in a way natural to her sex her words are not considered to be rekhtī. Pompilia in *The Ring and the Book* does not speak English rekhtī. He left also a collection of odes, elegies and lyrics, which is not extant, and a translation of *Iḥsān ul Qiṣaṣ*.

55. Shāh Muḥammad Qādrī, known also as Nūr i Daryā, became in 1673 successor to Amīn ud Dīn A'lā (No. 8). He was the author of some prose tracts containing Ṣūfī doctrines.

Urdu Literature in the Deccan Under the Mugals (1687–1730)

Two men bearing the name, 'Ājiz, viz. Muḥammad 'Alī 'Ājiz (No. 56) and 'Ārif ud Dīn 'Ājiz (No. 67) have sometimes been confused.

56. Muḥammad 'Alī 'Ājiz was the earlier writer; his style is simple, direct and forceful. He is author of a romance called *Qiṣṣa e Fīroz Shāh* or *Qiṣṣa e Malika i Miṣr* (1688 or earlier), 800 lines long, which deals with the story of the wife of Fīroz Shāh, King of Egypt. It is not known to what part of the country 'Ājiz belonged, but he was alive when Aurangzeb conquered the country in 1686 or 1687. (See p. 16.)

57. Valī Ullāh Qadrī, at the suggestion of his father,

translated *Ma'rifat i Sulūk* from the Persian original. The date is 1688.

58. SHEKH DĀŪD ẒA'IFĪ was a learned Ṣūfī who left two poems; one, a romance in the India Office Library, is without date or title (720 lines long); it tells the story of a woman who burnt herself alive because of her love for Muḥammad. Hindi words abound in it. The other is *Hidāyat i Hindī* (1689), a long work on the beliefs of the Ḥanafī sect.

59. BECĀRA flourished during Aurangzeb's time. We know only that he was a servant of the emperor and visited Delhi.

60. SHĀH HUSAIN ZAUQĪ, 'Bahr ul 'Irfān,' wrote in 1697 a poetical version of Vajhī's *Sab Ras* (see No. 24), which he called *Viṣāl ul 'Āshiqīn* or *Husn o Dil*, but it is much inferior to the prose original. He left also a number of other poems which have been lost, but MSS. of three works, a eulogy of 'Abd ul Qādir Jīlānī, *Mābāp Nāma*, and an account of the well-known Ṣūfī, Manṣūr, have been preserved.

61. AMĪN in 1697 composed a long poem which was a retelling of the ever popular *Yūsuf-Zulekhā*, mistakenly dated 1600–1 by Garcin de Tassy. He is not the same as Muḥammad Amīn (37) or Amīn (45).

62. QĀẒĪ MAḤMŪD BAḤRĪ was a prolific writer of Ṣūfī views, who flourished c. 1680–1700. He belonged to a village, Gogī, near Nuṣratābād, but went to Bijāpūr in 1684 and to Ḥaidarābād two years later. On one of his journeys he was attacked by robbers who destroyed all his writings. In 1700 however he wrote a romance called *Man Lagan* which has been printed. It contained so many difficult words that a glossary was prepared shortly after the work itself. It is now out of print. He left also fourteen love poems, four elegies, two odes, and a mystical ode called *Bangāb Nāma*.

63. MUḤAMMAD FAYYĀẒ VALĪ of Velūr (Vellore) is to be distinguished from his more famous contemporary and namesake of Aurangabad (No. 75). His time of activity is 1690–1707. He was the author of a romance, *Qiṣṣa e Ratn o Padm*, 8,000 lines long, based on Muḥammad Jāisī's *Padmāvat*,

which has been attributed to the other Valī, and of a collection of elegies, about 10,000 lines in all, called *Rauẓat ush Shuhadā*, 1707. His authorship of a short poem of 100 lines known as *Munājāt* is doubtful.

64 and 65. Maḥmūd Beg of Bījāpūr, and Fakhrī, a pupil of the Valī just mentioned, were friends who wrote in the end of the seventeenth century.

66. Aḥmad Gujrātī was a learned elegy writer in Aurangzeb's time. He knew Hindi, Persian, Arabic and Sanskrit.

67. 'Ārif ud Dīn 'Ājiz, a much more artificial writer than his namesake (No. 56); was the author of a romance named *Qiṣṣa e Lāl Gauhar* and of other extant poems. The poem written by the other 'Ājiz has been attributed to him, but the straightforward style in which it is written is a strong argument for believing that the earlier author wrote it. 'Ārif ud Dīn was born in north India. His father came from Balkh in the time of Aurangzeb, 1659–1707. He soon died, and the future poet was brought up by the second son of Āṣaf Jāh, the first Niẓām of Ḥaidarābād, whose dynasty is still on the throne. He went with his benefactor to Aurangābād and was given a salary sufficient for his simple wants.

68. Abu Ṭālib Ṭālib was a Ḥaidarābād poet who visited Delhi and lived there for some time. His date is the last decade of the seventeenth century.

69. Ṣabāī of Aḥmadābād (flor. c. 1695) has been compared in style with Naẓīr of Agra.

70. Shāh Bīr Ullāh Mujrimī in 1702 told poetically the story of Vajhī's *Sab Ras*, entitling it *Gulshan i Ḥusn i Dil*; as a poem it is mediocre, but it has the merit of brevity and simplicity.

71. 'Irāqī was another poet of that time.

72. Faqīr Ullāh Āzād, a contemporary of Valī Aurangābādī (No. 75), wrote with much pathos. This was the result of a disappointment in love which led to his wandering restlessly till he reached Delhi. Little is known of his writings.

73. Maḥbūb 'Ālam, known as Shekh Jīvan (flor. circ. 1720) wrote several poems, the chief of which are *Dard*

Nāma, 5,500 lines in length, and an elegy on the death of Muḥammad. In the latter the speakers are 'Āisha and Fāṭima. Others doubtfully attributed to him are *Maḥshar Nāma*, *Khvāb Nāma* and *Dahez Nāma*. He was a religious writer, probably a Dakhnī.

74. VAJDĪ (about 1710) wrote a long romance, *Tuḥfa e 'Ashiqīn*, based on, or adapted from, Farīd ud Dīn 'Aṭṭār's Persian work *Khusrau Nāma*. The romance is extant, but owing to some confusion between this Vajdī and another who lived a century earlier, the authorship is not beyond doubt.

75. **Vali.** SHAMS UD DĪN VALĪ ULLĀH (1667–1741) is one of the greatest names in Urdu literature. He was born and brought up in the Deccan. His actual birthplace was Aurangābād and he is often referred to as Valī Aurangābādī, a name which distinguishes him from Valī Velūrī or Dakhnī (No. 63). Little or nothing is known of his family, but he is supposed by some to have been descended from Gujrat ancestors, and possibly connected with the famous saint Vajīh ud Dīn. When he was about 20 he went to Gujrat to complete his education, and he always retained a warm affection for the country, particularly for Sūrat, as his poem in praise of that town shows. While he was studying in Gujrat he became very much attached to a Sayyid called Abu'l Ma'ālī, with whom he travelled to Delhi, perhaps in 1700. There he placed himself under the spiritual direction of Sa'd Ullāh Gulshan to whom he showed his verses. He must already have written a considerable amount of Dakhnī verse, for he lived among Dakhnī poets with a long line of nearly a hundred Dakhnī poets behind him, whose works must have been familiar to him, but now probably his teacher, seeing how excellent his Dakhnī verses were, advised him to give up Persian altogether.

We are not quite sure of the sequence of events or of individual dates. He no doubt recited his Urdu poems before the poets of Delhi. These men whose vernacular was Urdu were writing poetry solely in Persian, unaware of the fact that for nearly 400 years prose and verse had been written in Urdu; but they were immensely impressed by the facility with which Valī expressed his thoughts in that language. His verses became so popular that people began to sing them in the bazaar and he was everywhere received with honour. Valī's visit to Delhi created a revolution in the poetry of north India. After a time he revisited his native land, but returned again in 1722 to Delhi, a city of which he was very fond. This time he took with him all his poems and his triumph was complete. He died in Aḥmadābād in 1741. Valī's writings may be divided linguistically into three sections, viz. pure Dakhnī, about a third of the whole; ordinary Urdu but with many Dakhnī words; pure Urdu. His lyrics number 422 and take up about three quarters of his collection; he wrote six odes dealing with religious subjects or eulogising saints; two maṡnavīs, one being in praise of Sūrat; and a number of poems in other styles. He wrote no long poems, and he never wrote encomiums on earthly rank or greatness. One poem traditionally attributed to him, *Dah Majlis* or *Rauẓat ush Shuhadā*, is by the other Valī (No. 63).

His style was simple and dignified, sometimes rising to real eloquence; he was essentially a religious man of a mystical cast of thought, and his writings present a vivid picture of the life of the time. He ranks probably in the first half-dozen Urdu poets, and his importance as being the man who induced the Delhi poets to write in their native language can hardly be over-rated. In the days when the wealth of early Dakhnī poetry was not known, he received the title of *Bābā e Rekhta*, Father of Urdu; and so far as his relationship to Delhi is concerned he almost deserves it.

Valī's Younger Contemporaries in the Deccan

The early Deccan period of Urdu ends approximately when the Delhi period begins (between 1735 and 1740) but in speaking of Dakhnī poets we must for the sake of convenience include some who were still writing when Urdu poetry began in Delhi.

Elegies on the death of Ḥasan, Ḥusain and their families are an important feature of Urdu poetry; they began in the Deccan, and Qulī Quṭb Shāh (No. 20) was the first elegy writer. His example was followed by others, especially in Bījāpūr, where most of the kings were Shi'ahs and therefore encouraged margiya writing.

A valuable MS. in Edinburgh University Library contains 238 elegies by Hāshim 'Alī and 289 by sixty-three other Dakhnī authors, some of whom are not mentioned in any extant book or MS. elsewhere. It shows the existence of a school of elegy writers of no little merit. They are, it is true, limited in their outlook, as they confine themselves to one or two incidents in the Karbalā story and avoid all embellishment of the narrative. Their date is the first half of the eighteenth century. The best are given below.

76. Hāshim 'Alī (c. 1680–1760) probably of Gujrat, is the author of a large collection of elegies entitled *Dīwān i Husainī*. He lived in Burhānpūr during the years 1721–46. Internal evidence shows that the date given in the MS. just referred to is wrong. He was a writer of considerable power. Some have confused him with Mīrāṉ Hāshimī of Bījāpūr, who died in 1697 (No. 54).

Other writers whose elegies are found in the MS. are:

77. Imāmī; eight elegies, under 200 lines in all, showing picturesque, dramatic effects.

78. Razā of Gujrat, a good poet and famous teacher, who writes with great force; fifteen elegies, 720 lines.

79. Sayyid of Gujrat, also a vigorous writer; eight Dakhnī and two Persian elegies.

80. Gulāmī of Gujrat; seventeen elegies, 760 lines; a strongly imaginative and powerful writer who introduced interesting dialogues into his elegies—perhaps the only old author to do so; he had a good use of language.

81. Qādir (about 1736); seventeen elegies, 610 lines; he belonged to the Deccan, probably Haidarābād, and seems to have died before 1740. He wrote with pathos and feeling.

82. Yatīm Aḥmad of Burhānpūr, sometimes wrongly called Gulām Aḥmad, left seven short elegies of an average length of under 50 lines. The best is the fifth in which Ḥusain's wife describes the death of their one year old child Asgar 'Alī.

83. Sayyid Ashraf Ashraf (1713) is a very fair poet. A MS. has been discovered which contains a romance

translated by him in 1713, entitled *Jang Nāma e Ḥaidarī*, an account of the victories of 'Alī. It is 1,612 lines long. Thirteen of his elegies are found in the Edinburgh MS.

84. MU'TABIR KHĀN 'UMR (c. 1730), a pupil of Valī Dakhnī (No. 63), was an elegy writer some of whose elegies are in the MS. just mentioned.

85. SAYYID MUḤAMMAD VĀLIḤ is the author of a tragic romance called *Qiṣṣa e Ṭālib o Mohanī*, a poetical version of a story said to have been related by an old Brahman from the Koṅkaṇ. The date is probably about 1720.

86. **Siraj.** SIRĀJ UD DĪN (1714–63) was the greatest of the poets who clustered round Valī Aurangābādī (No. 75). He belonged to Aurangābād where he was educated. At that time the town was full of life and gaiety. Aurangzeb had spent his last days there and it was the home of many writers and scholars. Sirāj was acknowledged as a fitting successor to Valī, and the people who gathered week by week for the poetical meetings held in his house said that they were enjoying the fruit of Valī's plants which had been tended and watered by Sirāj. He belonged to the Cishtī sect and was even more of a mystic than Valī. First he wrote in Persian, but he gave it up for Urdu. His *Dīwān* contains about 10,000 lines, made up chiefly of lyrics and romances. His second volume was called his *Kulliyāt*, and in addition to these he wrote a romance entitled *Bostān i Khayāl*. His poetry is characterised by freshness of subject and loftiness of thought, while his language is a source of astonishment on account of its resemblance to the Urdu of to-day. Ṣūfīs in particular found spiritual food in his writings. One of his romances under the guise of a story about a rose and a nightingale discusses the attainment of divine knowledge. He became famous during his lifetime and attracted many pupils.

87. GULĀM QĀDIR SĀMĪ (1695–1782) was a popular poet with a considerable reputation. He was much esteemed as a teacher of poetics and used to go on tour to meet his pupils. His chief work is a long romance, *Qiṣṣa e Sarv Shimshād*, which is about 10,000 lines in length. His writings, though full of similes and allusions, are simple, elegant and clear. He was brought up in Aurangābād and died there.

88. SAYYID MUḤAMMAD is the author of a romance called *Faiẓ i 'Ām* written in 1727.

89. MIRZĀ DĀŪD DĀŪD (d. 1754), like most Dakhnī poets of his time, was born and brought up in Aurangābād; he was a pupil of Valī Aurangābādī and was much influenced by him. His *dīvān* is short, containing only 1,000 lines.

90. ṢĀBIR in 1743 wrote a short romance of 250 lines on the duties of husband and wife. It is not known in what part of the Deccan he lived.

91. 'ABD UL ḤAĪ KHĀN ṢĀRIM (1729–58) was the first Vazir of Āṣaf Jāh, Nizam of Ḥaidarābād. We know only that he was a poet and died young.

92. SAYYID 'ABDULLĀH QIYĀSĪ was the author of an unnamed romance, telling the story of a merchant and his wife.

III

THE FIRST CENTURY OF URDU POETRY IN DELHI (A.D. 1730-1830)

The Emperors Akbar, Jahāngīr, Shāhjahān, and Aurangzeb reigned one after another from 1556 to 1707. After the death of Aurangzeb the power of the Mugal Empire declined, and within a few years there were two wars of succession. In 1707 Aurangzeb's eldest son defeated his brothers and came to the throne, taking the name of Bahādur Shāh. His short reign of five years was disturbed by war with the Sikhs whose military power had been consolidated by the tenth Guru, Govind Singh (1675–1708). On Bahādur Shāh's death in 1712, another war of succession took place. Then Jahāndār reigned for 11 months (1712–13) and Farrukhsiyar for six years (1713–19). For the next twenty years the country round Delhi enjoyed at least comparative peace, which was rudely broken in 1739 by the invasion of Nādir Shāh, 'the greatest warrior Persia ever produced.' Muhammad Shāh came to the throne in 1719 and retained his position till 1748. He was not a great or good ruler, but he was a patron of the arts, and during these twenty years of peace, poets assembled in Delhi.

The empire however began to break up. During 1724 Āṣaf Jāh made himself independent in the Deccan, founding the dynasty which still rules there; and in the same year Oudh (Avadh) practically ceased to recognise the authority of the capital. Shortly afterwards the Panjab and Bengal passed out of the Emperor's control. Aḥmad Shāh reigned from 1748 to 1754 when he was blinded and deposed; he was succeeded by 'Ālamgīr II who was murdered in 1759. Shāh 'Ālam reigned without power from 1759 to 1806.

Aḥmad Shāh Durrānī of Persia (not to be confounded with his namesake the Emperor) invaded India repeatedly between 1748 and 1761. The Marathas were at the zenith of their power in 1758, and between that year and 1804 made frequent attacks on Delhi or the Panjab. The exodus of poets from Delhi, several times alluded to below, will be understood if we realise how often it was the scene of bloody conflicts. In 1739 it was captured by Nādir Shāh, in 1756 by Aḥmad Shāh Durrānī, in 1760 by the Marathas, and in 1788 by the Rohilla chieftain, Gulām Qādir, who blinded the Emperor. General Lake defeated Sindhia at the battle of Delhi in 1803, and Holkar unsuccessfully attacked the city in 1804.

The chief Persian poets at the court of Muḥammad Shāh (1719–48) were Mu'izz ud Dīn Fiṭrat, Qazilbāsh Khān Ummed, Sulaimān Qulī Khān Vidād, Sa'd Ullāh Gulshan, Murtazā Qulī Khān Firāq, Shams ud Dīn Faqīr, 'Abd ul Qādir Bedil, 'Alī Qulī Khān Nadīm and Sirāj ud Dīn 'Alī Khān Ārzū. They all wrote in Persian, but occasionally amused themselves by writing couplets partly or wholly in Urdu. Sometimes one line was Urdu and one Persian, sometimes half a line was Persian and half Urdu; or the verbs and prepositions might be Persian and the other words Urdu, or the nouns and adjectives Persian and the rest Urdu. This was not true Urdu poetry. These men, therefore, are for the most part rightly excluded from our survey. One of them, however, Ārzū, deserves mention, for he was the instructor of Mīr Taqī and a number of other poets. To understand this we must remember that Urdu poetry followed the rules of Persian prosody, and a Persian might give good advice even though his knowledge of Urdu was slight. Ārzū was a learned man and wrote admirable Persian verse. He was also the author of two Urdu dictionaries, *Navādir ul Farẓ* and *Garāib ul Lugāt*.

Gradually a love for Urdu, the home language, grew up, and poets began to feel the absurdity of speaking one language and writing another. Further, they had heard of poets in the Deccan and seen some of their poetry. But the culminating influence was the visit to Delhi of Dakhnī poets such as Valī, Firāqī, Fakhrī and Āzād. In particular, the importance of Valī's coming to Delhi cannot be over-estimated. He was far the greatest of the living Dakhnī poets, and he was able to show the Delhi poets not only how poetry could be written in Urdu, but to tell them that he was only one of a long line of Dakhnī writers in both prose and poetry. He appears to have visited Delhi first in 1700 and again in 1722. As we have already seen, even the street urchins used to go about reciting his verses. The Urdu poetry of north India was born very shortly after 1722; soon there were scores of poets writing it. Mīr Taqī's anthology, compiled in 1752, contains the names of 70 Delhi poets and 32 from the Deccan and Gujrat. The process of Persianisation now received a great impetus. Persian writers became the sole models. Persian words, idioms, images and sentiments were introduced, together with Persian history, geography and legends. What was called 'polishing' the language was really 'Persianising' it; poetry became more and more artificial and un-Indian. Persian gardens with Persian trees, fruits and flowers, were transplanted to India, while Persian scenery and customs, even Persian heroes and heroines, found a new home there. We had something similar in our own country, though to a very much more limited extent, when our poets wrote of nymphs, fauns, satyrs, naiads and muses, or of Olympus with its gods and goddesses, or of Elysium and celestial ambrosia.

In Urdu everything now became foreign, artificial and exotic. Urdu critics have themselves often admitted that the old Hindi poets were far truer to nature. To say that a garden was so beautiful that birds fainted in trying to fly over it conveys no meaning, but a few lines suggesting the beauty and perfume of the flowers gives a real picture of their loveliness.

This sterilising process, which had begun as far back as the time of Qulī Quṭb Shāh, was already well marked in Valī's later works; poetry became increasingly artificial to the time of Nāsikh (d. 1838) and his disciples, whose writings are little more than lists of correct idioms. Since then a healthy reaction has set in, and there is reason to hope that Urdu poetry will in the future more adequately fulfil its real function. As we shall see later on, the Lucknow school was even more artificial than the school of Delhi. There was always a tendency to use similes and metaphors for their own sake as mere flourishes, and this was carried to incredible lengths in Lucknow.

The most serious result of copying Persian writers was the introduction of debased forms of erotic sentiment. The earlier Delhi writers were nearly all Ṣūfīs, or wrote as if they were. Some people perverted pure Ṣūfī doctrines, and Ṣūfī terms of strong love towards a Divine object were used by men of polluted minds with an entirely different meaning. Such writings are now condemned by all thinking Indians and belong to a past age. We do not expect them to-day.

This chapter deals with a period of approximately a hundred years (1730–1830). The first part of it exhibits the features of the previous age. Poetry continued to be simple and natural; poets wrote of what they had seen and felt; metaphors and similes were unartificial and straightforward. There was no hankering after excessive ornament, for it was realised that beauty does not require to be adorned. The figure of speech known as *īhām*, playing on words, which is so common in Hindi literature, continued for a considerable time; it ceased only towards the end of the eighteenth century.

This period falls conveniently into three parts, associated specially with the names of (1) Ḥātim, (2) Mīr, Saudā and Dard, (3) Insha, Muṣḥafī and Naẓīr; but the sections overlap, and the poets of the third were young contemporaries of the poets of the first.

A. **The Age of Hatim** is characterised by pure, chaste and effective language, by poetical vigour and fervour, and by monotonous sameness of subject, the theme of love pervading nearly all that was written. Plays on words were common; similes and metaphors were few. Most of the writers were Ṣūfīs.

B. **The Age of Mazhar, Sauda, Mir and Dard.** The language assumed a new power—the gold was being refined, the sapling became a sturdy tree, the boy became a man. Ṣūfī influence continued strong. This is the time of the 'Four Pillars of Urdu,' Maẓhar, Saudā, Mīr and Dard. The poets had nothing new to say, they therefore devoted themselves to elaborating the old subjects; they remained in their garden, not venturing outside the gates, but giving themselves to intensive cultivation within. Owing to the unscientific habit of arranging poetry according to alphabetic or other arbitrary order, it is not possible to follow the development of thought or language in the case of individual writers. When we remember that some of them lived to a great age—Mīr was 86 when he died—we realise how much we have lost.

C. **The Age of Mushafi, Insha and Nazir.** There was no real advance in this period; old subjects were re-arranged and there was much more humour. A regrettable feature is the introduction of reḵẖtī (pp 30, 54).

The greatest poets who come into this chapter are perhaps first Mīr, then Saudā and Naẓīr, lastly Mīr Ḥasan and Dard. The greatest single poems are Mīr Ḥasan's romances, *Siḥr ul Bayān* and *Gulzār i Iram*, and Aṡar's *Ḵẖvāb o Ḵẖayāl*.

A. THE AGE OF ḤĀTIM

We now turn to the Age of Ḥātim, first noting the names of Afẓal and Zaṭallī, two writers who lived before Urdu poetry properly began in Delhi.

93. Muḥammad Afẓal (d 1625) belonged either to the Deccan or to Jhanjhāna near Meraṭh (Meerut). He was the author of a remarkable *Bārah Māsā* (600 lines long) in Hindi metres and full of Hindi sentiment. It tells of Hindu life and festivals, and is entirely Indian. Yet it is permeated with Persian expressions. The picture of the lonely wife talking to her companions about her absent husband corresponds to that found in many Hindi poems. A Dakhnī poet called Afẓal, possibly the same man, wrote a glowing account of the life of the saint 'Abd ul Qādir Jīlānī.

94. Mīr Ja'far Zaṭallī or Zaṭalī (1659–1713) was a confirmed jester, and so was named Zaṭallī (jester) by one of the princesses. He wrote satires on nearly everybody, not sparing even Aurangzeb's sons. He accompanied one of these sons, Kām Baḵẖsh, to the Deccan, where perhaps he

received his first poetic inspiration. Most of his verse is Persian, but his Urdu verses show remarkable vigour and freshness. His description of the turmoil following the death of Aurangzeb is a fine piece of writing. Though full of Persian words it does not show Persian influence in thought. His autobiographical poem, *Sulūk*, 200 lines in length, shows the same characteristics. He is also the author or collector of a number of proverbs. For his prose see No. 182. He seems to have been put to death by the Emperor Farru<u>kh</u>siyar.

THE DEATH OF AURANGZEB

By Mīr Ja'far Zatallī

(After Aurangzeb's death his sons A'ẓam and Mu'aẓẓam engaged in internecine warfare to obtain the throne; Mu'aẓẓam was successful.)

1. Where shall we find so excellent a king,
2. Complete, consummate, perfect, knowing hearts?
3. The world is weeping tears of blood,
4. And gentle sleep to no one comes
5. Because of cannon's noise and guns.
6. Men carrying goods and guns upon their heads,
7. And fleeing here and there on every side;
8. Beds on their heads, and children in their arms.
9. Cutting, smiting on all sides
10. Wrenching, splitting on all sides
11. On all sides death and violence.
12. Turmoil, axes, daggers, poniards!
13. That side A'ẓam, this Mu'aẓẓam.
14. Fighting, struggling, both I find.
15. But let me see whom God approves as king!
16. For whom the faithful offer Friday prayers.

95. Aḥmad, of whom nothing is known, is the author of the following beautiful poem, found in a MS. notebook dated 1748. The date of the poem may be put provisionally at 1650–1700.

A VISION OF DEATH

By Aḥmad

1. When passed the night and came the day,
   'Twas then I understood.
2. Ere I had been one hour awake,
   Ah, then I understood.

3. When I had drunk the cup of death,
My eyes were opened then;
4. When on the bier my corpse they placed,
'Twas then I understood.
5 I nothing recked of covering quilt or cloth.
6. When 'neath my head the stone they placed,
'Twas then I understood.
7. What time my friends left me and went,
They left me quite alone.
8. Munkir, Nakīr, both questioned me,
'Twas then I understood.
9. When came the time of my account,
My eyes were opened then;
10. I read the statement of my works;
'Twas then I understood.
11. My life was spent, the whole of it,
No work had I to show.
12. When passed the noonday of my life,
'Twas then I understood.
13. Save God and the apostle now,
On Aḥmad's side was none;
14. But when I trusted grace divine,
'Twas then I understood.

96. Najm ud Dīn (Shāh Mubārak) Ābrū (c. 1692–1747) really belonged to Lucknow, but went to Delhi when quite young and spent his life there. His first and chief collection was lost in the Mutiny, but a shorter one, perhaps containing selections from the other, is said to be extant. He was also the author of a good romance, entitled *Mauʿiẓa e Ārāish i Maʿshūq*. His importance lies principally in the fact that he led the way and had a number of pupils. He indulged in a good deal of punning, but wrote good, idiomatic Urdu.

97. Muḥammad Shākir Nājī died in 1754 at an early age. He was a poet of great promise, whose career was prematurely cut short. Only ten lines survive out of a long poem in five lined stanzas (*mukhammas*) which used to be greatly admired. It was written just after Nādir Shāh's invasion in 1739 and vividly describes that event and the desolation it created. It pictures clearly the life of those times. Owing to the excessive use of metaphors his style is very difficult, but people like his clever, critical verses, and the work which he left acquired considerable popularity.

It has not been published. He was irritable, quarrelsome, facetious and sarcastic.

98. SHARF UD DĪN MAẒMŪN (b. before 1689, d. about 1745) belonged to Jajmaū near Agra, but went early to Delhi. He was a pupil of Ārzū who called him the Toothless Poet, owing to his having lost all his teeth. Only 400 lines of his verse are extant; they are filled with out of the way words and phrases, artificial metaphors and unsavoury insinuations. He lived as a *darvesh* in a mosque, but originally was a soldier.

99. MUṢṬAFĀ KHĀN YAKRANG, one of the earliest Delhi poets, was a contemporary of Maẓmūn. He left a volume of love-poems in the Ṣūfī style, interpreted in different ways according to the taste of the reader, and an elegy. He was regarded as a very accomplished poet.

100. **Hatim.** ẒUHŪR UD DĪN HĀTIM (b. 1699, d. 1781 or 1792) was the greatest but one of the Delhi poets who preceded Saudā and Mīr. Under Valī's powerful influence he set himself to write Urdu poetry in which he was very successful. He had a clear, natural and eloquent style. His first volume, the *Dīvān*, which was very large, was in the old manner, full of punning. Later on he wrote another book in which he inserted selections from his first, giving it the name of *Dīvānzāda*, 'son of the Dīvān.' The subject matter is that mixture of erotic and Ṣūfī sentiment, which is found in so many of the early Urdu writers. He became famous as the teacher of others, and in the interesting Persian preface to the *Dīvānzāda* he claims 45 pupils, one of them being no less a personage than Saudā. He tells us about the Hindi words and expressions which he had given up, and the Arabic or Persian words which he had employed, and excuses himself for following the popular fancies in certain spellings. He winds up with a pious hope that 'Please God, no inelegant word will be found' in the new and selected *Dīvān*, though he admits that in the former, larger one, he had many words and idioms which he now dislikes. It includes those elegies, romances and lyrics from his larger work which he considered most worth preserving.

101. MUḤAMMAD AḤSAN AḤSAN was a contemporary poet of whom next to nothing is known. A few lines of

his which are extant show that he used an early form of the language.

B. THE AGE OF THE 'FOUR PILLARS OF URDU' —MAẔHAR, SAUDĀ, MĪR, AND DARD

102. **Mazhar.** Mirzā Jān Jānān Maẓhar (1699–1781) was the greatest of the Delhi poets before Saudā and Mīr. His father was in the service of the Emperor Aurangzeb, but died when Maẓhar was hardly more than a boy. Until he was thirty years of age he lived in enclosures containing the tombs of holy men. It was during this time that he came under Ṣūfī influence. He was a man of hasty temper, but very friendly and jovial; rather faddy and very independent; after becoming an ascetic he refused all rewards, declining even large sums of money. Living as a *darvesh*, he had pupils in the art of poetry, and religious disciples who received spiritual instruction from him. His death was tragic: being a strong Sunnī he once unguardedly expressed disapproval of something in the Muḥarram procession, with the result that he was shot during the night. He lingered a day or two but refused to describe his murderer. He is reverenced as a *shahīd* or martyr.

Āzād calls him one of the Four Pillars of Urdu; his reputation in Urdu is surprising, for only a few score of his couplets are extant; but his language was so clear and limpid and his Persian constructions so pleasing to the people of his time that he was awarded a very high position.

103. **Sauda.** Muḥammad Rafī' Saudā (1713–80) was formerly considered the greatest of Urdu poets. Even now some readers of the old school would give him that rank. He is best discussed in connection with his great contemporary, Mīr Taqī Mīr (p. 49). Saudā was born and brought up in Delhi, where he lived till life became almost unbearable. Nādir Shāh's invasion was a thing of the past, but Aḥmad Shāh's repeated attacks from the north took place when Saudā was in the prime of life, and on the south were the Marathas, anxious to get all they could out of the city. Nearly all Urdu poets left Delhi, one after the other. Saudā went to Farrukhābād (c. 1665) and, on the death of the Navāb in 1771, to Faizābād where Shujā'ud Daula then lived. Āṣaf

ud Daula succeeded him in 1775 and moved his court to Lucknow. Saudā went with him, was given a pension and received the title of Malik ush Shu'arā, King of Poets.

It has been said that he was the first to write odes and satires, and certainly it was he who first wrote them with power. He and Ẕauq are the greatest ode writers in Urdu, and no one has approached him in satire. He was a good writer of elegies and is surpassed only by those who, like Anīs and Dabīr, have made a speciality of elegies. His didactic poems and lyrics are numerous, but those forms of verse did not suit his temperament; he also wrote many riddles in verse. Such riddles are common in Hindi, and some are attributed to Amīr Khusrau. Saudā's are very good, but we cannot give the name of 'poetry' to that form of verbal juggling. Happily his example has not been followed.

Saudā's poetical works may be divided as follows: (i) over 40 odes, a majority of them in praise of nawābs, about a third celebrating Muḥammad and his relatives, the rest purely satirical; (ii) nearly 100 elegies with an average of 100 lines each; and (iii) a large number of lyrics, containing perhaps 10,000 lines in all. There are also a number of other short poems in various forms.

He used to go about with a servant named Ḡunca who carried pen and ink. When annoyed he called at once for his writing materials, and there and then, whether at home or in the street, began a savage satire against the object of his annoyance; and there were few bold enough to risk his anger.

His odes are regarded as equal to the best Persian odes, on the ground that in force of language he is superior to Anvarī and Khāqānī, while he puts 'Urfī and Ẓuhūrī to shame with his delicate imagination. He was greater as an Urdu writer than as a poet. He had a power, not equalled by any other Urdu poet, of making words do his bidding; he stands alone in his manipulation of the language, which he raised to a new pinnacle. (See No. 184.)

103a. Ashraf 'Alī Khān Fiḡān (d. 1772), a foster brother of the Emperor Aḥmad Shāh, only second rate as a poet, but very clever and witty, was famed for the excellence of his Urdu. He left one volume of poems.

104. **Mīr.** Muḥammad Taqī Mīr (1724–1810) belonged

to Agra, but on the death of his father went to Delhi where he lived till 1783. When he forsook it he went by invitation to Oudh. The story that leaving home in poverty he reached Lucknow unknown, and took part in a poetical meeting with such effect that he was at once recognised and received with honour, is untrue. He remained in Lucknow till his death. His sense of his importance made him decry others. A famous dictum of his is on record that at that time only Saudā and he were real poets, Dard was half a poet, and Soz a quarter. He wrote an ode called *Ajgarnāma*, the Dragon Story, in which he represented himself as a huge serpent swallowing up other poets, who appear as rats, snakes, scorpions and centipedes. Allowance must be made for him; his life was embittered and sad, he had been disappointed in love and was very poor. Naturally proud, he was rendered still prouder by misfortune. After he left Delhi things were better, for the Navābs of Oudh were very kind to him, but he was so touchy that he quarrelled with his benefactors. Āzād's stories about these matters are doubtless exaggerated, but they are not wholly false.

Mīr was at his best in lyrics and romances; his lyrics, in fact, have rarely been equalled. In romances he has few equals and only one superior, viz. Mīr Ḥasan. The impassioned *vāsokht* may be regarded as a sub-division of the lyric. In this form of verse, which he was the first to write in Urdu, he has never been surpassed. All these suited his tender and sad nature. But he was unfitted for the splendour of the ode, and his odes are poor; elegies he hardly attempted. He was not a court poet, and like Valī, Dard and Ātish, had an aversion to writing panegyrics of great men. When Dr. Gilchrist was beginning his work in Fort William College, Mīr was thought of as a possible translator, but was passed over on account of his great age.

He wrote several volumes of lyrics containing between 30,000 and 40,000 lines, and a large number of romances. Those on which his great fame rests deal with love; they are *Shu'la e 'Ishq* translated into prose by Saudā, and *Daryā e 'Ishq*; his *Sāqī Nāma* on Spring is nearly as good, though shorter, and *Josh i 'Ishq* is also good. The others do not attain the same level, most of them are short.

He was very fond of keeping animals and wrote several poems about them, but they do not reach a high standard of excellence. One was on a dog and a cat, another on a goat, another on the death of his cock, and another on a kitten called Mānī.

Some of his poems are on natural phenomena such as heavy rain, which on one occasion brought down his house, and on another spoilt a journey which he was making; one was on his search for a livelihood, and one on 'Lying'; he wrote one on Navāb Āṣaf ud Daula's hunting. His *Tazhīk ul Khayāl*, professedly on the greatness of poetry, is actually a personal attack on a young man. His *Ajgarnāma* has been mentioned above. Some of his love poems are inferior; such are *Mu'āmalāt i 'Ishq*, and *I'jāz i 'Ishq*.

He wrote in beautiful, simple, almost conversational language, but he is unequal. His best is the best that Urdu possesses. One critic has said *pastash bagāyat past, balandash bisyār baland*—'his depths are extremely low, his heights very high.'

Sauda and Mir. These two great writers were contemporaries and lived for long in the same town, Delhi; but they were a complete contrast to each other in both character and style. Mīr was sad, tender, gloomy and poor; Saudā living in comfortable circumstances, was jovial and boisterous, taking a cheerful view of life. Mīr was very retiring, and disliked courts and court life; Saudā revelled in public assemblies and loved courts; he was a thorough man of the world. Mīr's writing was characterised by simple language, full of pathos and emotion; Saudā wrote with vigour and grandeur. Like Marlowe, he had a 'mighty line,' sometimes his style was turgid. Mīr at his best was the better poet, but Saudā was the greater master of Urdu. From these differences it follows naturally that Mīr excelled in poems of love, lyrics and romances, while Saudā's best efforts were in his odes or panegyrics and in his bitter satires. Mīr's sole panegyric is not worth reading, his odes are poor, and his satire, the *Ajgar Nāma*, cannot be compared with his better work; similarly when Saudā writes lyrics he is always in danger of bursting their bonds and changing them into odes, and his romances are of inferior quality. The success of his elegies lay not in their pathos, but in their descriptions of battles and scenery.

One writer has remarked acutely that every age of Urdu has had its pair of poets: one natural, who wrote from the heart, the other artificial, writing more for effect. He mentioned the following writers, the first in each case being the natural poet: Mīr and Saudā, Mushafī and Inshā, Ātish and Nāsikh, Gālib and Zauq, Dāg and Amīr.

105. MUHAMMAD HUSAIN KALĪM (fl. 1750) was an author who wrote both verse and prose. He translated into Urdu a difficult Arabic work called *Fuṣūṣ ul Ḥikm*, and wrote a little treatise on Hindi prosody and rhyme. His collection contains a large number of poems in the more usual forms. His poetry has never been popular; Mīr Ḥasan says because it 'lacks salt,' but Mīr says it is too difficult; the fact is he had a style of his own, and people did not like it. Practically no facts about his life are known. (See No. 183a.)

106. QIYĀM UD DĪN QĀIM (d. between 1787 and 1795) belonged to Cāndpūr, but lived in Delhi till the troubles compelled him to leave. He had several teachers and quarrelled with them all. He was a man of strong imaginative power with a good style, and by some has been regarded as nearly equal to Saudā. His poems include very many lyrics and a number of odes, some eulogistic, others satirical. He wrote also some romances such as *Maṣnavī i 'Ishq i Darvesh*, *Ḥairat Afzā* and *Ramz uṣ Ṣalāt*. His pupil, Kamāl, put him as second only to Saudā among the poets of the century; Shefta, however, regards that statement as absurd. He was the author of a Persian anthology of Urdu poets, entitled *Makhzan i Nikāt* (1754). Perhaps his greatest success was in quatrains. His poems were published in 1927.

107. **Dard**. MĪR DARD (1719–1785), one of the Four Pillars of Urdu (p. 41), and one of the greatest of Urdu poets, was a Ṣūfī who wrote only religious lyrics and other poems of that type. He never wrote odes, romances or satires, and he avoided all praise of men, for his life was one of absorption in the duties of religion. All through the period of trouble which lasted forty years, he remained in Delhi, the only well known poet who did so.

He gave up soldiering to become a *darvesh*. When a mere boy he began writing religious prose tracts. We know the names of a dozen of his prose works, mostly dealing with matters of religion. Like many Ṣūfis of the time he was musical and one of his tracts is entitled *Ḥurmat i Ġinā*, the Honour of Singing (not *Ġanā*, wealth, as sometimes stated). These tracts are all in Persian. As a lyric writer he has perhaps never been surpassed in Urdu; his verses were so keen and trenchant that they were likened to sharp swords, and were it not that he wrote almost altogether in one style he would rank with the two or three greatest poets in the language. When he died, one of his disciples said, 'Alas! gone from the world is God's beloved.'

108. MUḤAMMAD MĪR SOZ (1720–98) belonged to Delhi, where he was brought up. He first called himself Mīr, but changed his name to Soz because Mīr Taqī was already known as Mīr. He was noted for his strength of arm, his archery and his calligraphy. In his youth he was extremely worldly, but when he was about 57 he completely changed his mode of life and thought. He was very poor and made several unsuccessful attempts to secure a regular income sufficient to live upon. He left Delhi in 1777 and after wandering from place to place, settled in Lucknow in 1797 where he died the following year. He cannot be called a great poet, though he had a considerable command of language, chose his words well and always wrote very pure, idiomatic and simple Urdu. His poetry is a collection of beautiful and charming words, with little thought behind them; *vox et praeterea nihil*. He did not write much; about 7,200 lines are extant. Apart from his lyrics he left between 40 and 50 quatrains which are in the same style and marked by the same excellence. His two romances are inferior.

He was a wonderful reciter and his voice was full of pathos; as he recited he acted with intense realism. On one occasion he so vividly acted a passage referring to a snake that the audience rose up in alarm, and on another he was so overcome by his self induced emotion that he fainted on the floor.

109. ṢANĀ ULLĀH KHĀN FIRĀQ was a pupil of Dard (No.

107) and belonged to Delhi, but his dates are not known exactly. He was a physician in his youth and acquired great fame in this connection. When he took up poetry he made very rapid progress, so that soon his name was as well-known for poetry as for medicine. Like most poets of those days he spent more time in polishing his verse than in developing his thought.

110. Aḥsan Ullāh K͟hān Bayān (d. 1798) belonged to Agra, but was born in Delhi. In old age he went to Ḥaidarābād, where he was employed during the last few years of his life. He was a poet who had a considerable flow of smooth, good, idiomatic language, not marked by much poetic power. There are several MS. copies of his poems.

111. Mīr Muḥammadī Bedār (d. between 1793 and 1797) belonged to Delhi and was a well-known member of the Cishtī sect. Only a little of his work has come down to us; it consists of lyrics of some merit.

112. Baqā Ullāh Baqā (d. 1791) was born in Delhi, though he came of an Agra family. He is better known for his quarrels with Mīr and Saudā than for his poetry, but his poetry, which is largely religious, shows him to have been no mean poet.

113. **Mir Hasan.** Mīr G͟hulām Ḥasan Ḥasan (b. about 1736, d. 1786) is one of the great names in Urdu poetry. He was born in Delhi, but during his boyhood went with his father to Faiẓābād, a place to which he became greatly attached. Some years later he went to Lucknow where he remained till his death. He is famous for his romance, *Siḥr ul Bayān*, often called simply *Mas̱navī e Mīr Hasan*, the most popular romance in Urdu. This was written within a year of his death. In idiomatic, simple and beautiful language it tells the story of the loves of Prince Benaẓīr and Badr Munīr. The idiom is strikingly like that of to-day. Largely on account of this poem, Mīr Ḥasan is considered the greatest romance writer in Urdu. He wrote ten other mas̱navīs, the best of which is *Gulzār i Iram* which praises Faiẓābād and satirises Lucknow; there is another on the same theme. Next after *Gulzār i Iram* in poetical power is the poem on the marriage of Āṣaf ud Daula. Two others speak of

Javāhir 'Alī Khān; one is on various kinds of Indian food; one, *Rumūz ul 'Ārifīn*, is religious; it is not of any poetic value. Most of his poems are comparatively short, but *Siḥr ul Bayān* is 4,442 lines long.

He wrote seven odes, panegyrics on navābs and other prominent men of the time; their poetic merit is small. He was, however, a good lyric writer; his collection of lyrics contains nearly 10,000 lines and has the same characteristics as his romances. He was also the author of an anthology in Persian which deals with 300 Urdu poets; in many points it is inaccurate. He had a great flow of language and a remarkable command of the best idiom; his style was sometimes ornate, but always clear.

C. THE AGE OF MUṢHAFĪ, INSHĀ, AND NAẒĪR

114. **Mushafi.** Ǥulām Hamadānī Muṣhafī (1750–1824) belonged to Amrohā, but went as a young man to Delhi, which he considered his native place. He was a writer of extraordinary fluency who could compose verse almost as he talked. In his poverty he used to compose on the spur of the moment and sell his poetry at so many lines a penny according to the willingness of the purchaser to pay. He wrote much more than has come down to us. If he had given more time to his composition he might have been a great poet, for in some of his writings there are signs of greatness. It has been said that he had an all-embracing mind, and could, when he chose, write like Saudā, Mīr, Soz, Inshā or Figān. He enjoyed a great reputation and had numerous pupils. He left no less than eight volumes of poetry. He was at his best in lyrics, but wrote also odes and romances. In the simplicity of his style he resembled Soz or Mīr, in his idioms Saudā. His purity of language was such that even to-day people turn with pleasure to read extracts from his works. His verse, which is very even in quality, is free from the obscenity which characterises so much of the verse of that age. Considering the circumstances of his writing there is a surprising amount of vigour and terseness in it. His last years were spent in quarrels with Inshā, but he found time in 1794 for the compilation of an important Persian anthology, dealing with 350 Urdu poets.

115. **Insha.** INSHĀ ALLĀH KHĀN INSHĀ (d. 1817), the great rival of Muṣḥafī, was one of the most remarkable figures in Urdu literature. He was a very clever man with an extremely good memory, and wrote in several languages. Until near the end of his life, when he was depressed by misfortune and poverty, he treated life as a joke; nearly everything he wrote was full of humour and sparkle. He was not so much a great poet as a brilliant writer. Born and brought up in Murshidābād, he went in 1786 to Delhi where the blind Emperor held his phantom court. Dissatisfied with his prospects he proceeded to Lucknow and there the Emperor's son, Sulaimān Shikoh, gave him assistance, and later the Navāb, Sa'ādat 'Alī Khān, and he became bosom friends. But his inveterate habit of joking was the cause of his undoing. In 1810 he ceased to be *persona grata* at court, indeed he was turned out of Lucknow, though afterwards permitted to return; and he spent the rest of his life in semi-confinement. Āzād's account is exaggerated; Inshā did not become insane or suffer the extreme poverty related, while the famous poem, which we are told fell like a bombshell in the Lucknow poetical assembly, was in reality written years before, in Delhi.

He had disagreements with other poets in Delhi, but when after his arrival in Lucknow he ousted Muṣḥafī as companion to Sulaimān Shikoh, a quarrel of great intensity broke out; the two poets abused each other in unmeasured language, while their patrons incited them to still greater efforts. Muṣḥafī was the natural poet, Inshā the clever, if somewhat artificial versifier (p. 50). Court life degraded his poetry, made it cleverer and more artificial, and took away its life. Yet when he liked he could write in a different style; his striking prayer beginning 'O merciful God! have mercy!' is an example of this. It is worthy of note that after he was ejected from the Lucknow court his poetry improved in sentiment and feeling. His writing is always characterised by brilliance, humour and versatility.

His chief collection is between 8,000 and 9,000 lines long; some of the lyrics are good, but there is little poetic feeling. His rekhtī poetry is extremely interesting, and, strangely enough, it is not obscene. Its linguistic value is considerable.

He was perhaps at his best in his odes, nine in all. The most famous of them is that on the Jubilee of George III, 1810. He wrote also some satirical poems which are not of great merit.

One of his most famous works is a Hindi prose story called *Kahānī Theṭh Hindī Meṅ*, in which no Arabic or Persian word is employed. His most striking work is contained in *Daryā e Laṭāfat* written in Persian. Part I, a treatise of the greatest interest on the Urdu language, is by Inshā, the second part, on prosody, is by his friend, Qatīl. We are here concerned only with Inshā's part; it is the first grammar of Urdu written by an Indian. He discusses not only Urdu grammar, but Urdu sounds and dialects, even individual peculiarities of pronunciation. Thus there was a certain Mīr Ġafr Ġainī who had a defect of speech; he used a uvular trill in place of the three sounds r, ṛ and l, and there is a long letter in which Inshā has written all the sounds as he pronounced them. In one respect Inshā was a century and a quarter ahead of his time. He recognised that the correct form of foreign words in Urdu, such as words from Arabic, is that used by ordinary men in daily conversation, not that found in the original language. (See No. 204.)

116. Ja'far 'Alī Ḥasrat, who died between 1791 and 1802, had many disciples, the most famous of whom was Jur'at (No. 117). He wrote with much simplicity and pathos. He was the author of two good sized collections of verse, about half given up to lyrics, and the remainder to odes, romances and shorter poems. One collection is much superior to the other. Āzād who seems to have read only the inferior one, speaks slightingly of him, saying that his poetry was like a tasteless sweet drink. He belonged to Delhi, but went to Lucknow. Near the end of his life he became a *darvesh*. He finally returned to Delhi and died there.

117. Qalandar Bakhsh Jur'at (d. 1810) belonged to Delhi, but was brought up in Faizābād. He went to Lucknow in 1810, when Inshā's quarrel with Muṣḥafī was at its height. He was essentially a *bon viveur*, and threw himself heartily into the life of the court. He wrote a large number of lyrics containing conventional descriptions of love, the kind of verse that one would expect from the life of

conviviality which he then lived. The language of the lyrics was elegant, but the sentiment was worthless. He did not write much, perhaps 20,000 lines in all. In addition to the lyrics and other poems of that kind he wrote some maṡnavis, one of some length on the coming of the rains in summer; another, half as long, called *Maṡnavī e Husn o 'Ishq*, a clever but artificial account of an amour.

118. Sa'ādat Yār Khān Rangīn (1756–1834) was a prolific writer in Urdu. He is notorious as the first writer of rekhtī, the language used by women, especially women of no reputation. Rekhtī verse has been described as a debased form of lyric invented by a debased mind in a debased age. The word 'rekhtī' is not employed for the *natural* speech of women; its usual meaning is Urdu verse written by a man as a *tour de force*, with the words and idioms common to women, including feminine genders; the man writes as if he were a woman, and in nearly every case does so with an evil motive. Urdu writers of to-day condemn rekhti as a deplorable product of the past, now fortunately never seen. It has been claimed that others wrote in rekhtī before Rangīn, but Inshā definitely asserts that Rangīn was the originator of it. Three names are associated with this kind of verse—Rangīn, Inshā and Jān Ṣāḥib (d. 1897). The last named exhibits it in its worst form, while the least objectionable rekhtī is to be found in Inshā, indeed in his case it has a real literary value. (See No. 54.)

Rangīn's works extend to many volumes. The following is a list. (1) *Nauratn i Rangīn* consisting of six collections of poetry, one being in rekhtī, and three prose works, one of which is Persian. (2) Several collections of maṡnavīs; he claimed he had written 46 with a total of 40,000 lines. The most famous of these is *Maṡnavī i Dilpażīr*; one was a treatise on the use of seven different kinds of weapons, another described the defeat of the Mugals by Mādhoji Sindhia, and another was on horses and their diseases. (3) Three prose works, viz. *Imtiḥān i Rangīn* (1820), which is an attempt to prove that he is the greatest of Urdu poets, and two collections of anecdotes about himself, valuable on account of the light they throw on the life of the time. One of them, *Majālis i Rangīn*, is in Persian and relates

65 stories, the other, *Akhbār i Rangīn*, in Urdu (1819), contains 93 stories. (4) Two odes translated from Arabic and a poem on Islām. (5) An ode transcribed from Saudā to which he added what he believed to be improvements. In his style there is polish and glitter, but not true poetic feeling. (See No. 205.)

119. In'ām Ullāh Khān Yaqīn (d. about 1850) is a poet who appears to have met with a violent death during the reign of Aḥmad Shāh (1748–54) at the age of 25. He was a great friend of Maghar, and some have said that the poetry attributed to Yaqīn was largely due to Maghar, but Kalim, who knew them both, denies this. It is more probable that the excellence of his poetry made people think that so young a man could not have written it. He was the author of a large number of very short lyrics in which love subjects are well handled. His language and thought are so attractive that some critics have believed he would have excelled Mīr and Saudā if he had lived longer.

120. **Asar.** Muḥammad Mīr Aṣar, was the brother of the famous Dard (No. 107). Like his brother and father he was a religious man and bore a great reputation for saintliness. He wrote many lyrics and a romance entitled *Khvāb o Khayāl*, which is very good.

121. Hidāyat Ullāh Khān Hidāyat (born c. 1730, d. 1800) was a poet much esteemed in his time. He has left nearly 20,000 lines of lyrics and some romances, the best of which is that in praise of Benares. He wrote also a short tract called *Cirag i Hidāyat*.

122. Qudrat Ullāh Qudrat (d. 1790) was born and brought up in Delhi, but left it in later life for Murshidābād, where he was very well received and enabled to live in comfort. Mīr thought very little of his ability, but others have spoken of him as a powerful writer.

123. Ẓiyā ud Dīn Ẓiyā of Delhi was a well-known poet who composed a highly esteemed volume of verse. He wrote lyrics, but did not care for odes or romances. He wandered from Delhi to Faiẓābād, Lucknow and Patna, where he was living near the end of the century. The exact time of his death is not certain. He was a very friendly man who entered fully into the joys and sorrows of others.

124. Ǥulām ʻAlī Rāsiḵh (1748–1822), who had not much connection with Delhi, comes in naturally at this point. He belonged to Patna, but moved about from place to place, visiting Ǥāzīpūr, Calcutta, Delhi and Lucknow. In 1807 he returned to his native place where he lived till his death. He wrote fourteen romances and many odes and lyrics; his style, though much admired for its simplicity and purity, is a little monotonous. Much of his writing gives expression to Ṣūfī doctrines.

125. **Nazir.** Valī Muḥammad Naẕīr (1740–1830) was thought little of during his lifetime, and for many years after his death, but thanks to a change in critical taste is now given a place in the first six or seven Urdu poets, ranking alongside of Saudā. Compared with the poets of his time he is unconventional, and does not follow the usual Persian methods; rejecting the images loved of Persian poets he prefers to describe the country he lives in with its people and their interests. The use of recondite Persian conceits and unnecessary Persian words was to him anathema. He freely employed Hindi words and spoke of Hindu as well as Muḥammadan affairs.

Not much of his work has been printed; he never wrote long poems; the longest in his first volume has under 450 lines, and nearly all have under 200 lines. He was a man who loved his country and people and gave himself to describing daily sights and scenes. At one time he was a schoolmaster, and several of his poems deal with subjects of interest to boys. Among these may be mentioned, in addition to those on boyhood and kite-flying, poems on animals such as the young squirrel, the bear cub, the wild buffalo and the little bird, the crow and the deer, keeping pigeons, the story of the goose and the birds, bulbul-fighting, and finally the short poem with the names of many birds which night and morning offer praise to God. A number of poems speak of festivals, chiefly Hindu; natural phenomena, especially dark nights and rainy days; articles of food; common objects like cowries or pice or household utensils; everyday subjects such as poverty, money, flattery, good and evil, old age, youth, swimming, dreams, death, generosity; ordinary people like *faqīrs*, astrologers or merchants;

some describe scenes in Agra; one deals with the boyhood of Krishna; lastly he has eleven poems on Muslim religious subjects from which lines are often quoted by *faqīrs* to this day.

In early life he was licentious, but as he grew older he changed and became the thoughtful moralist whom we now know. He was not a courtier, he neither eulogised the rich nor lampooned those of humbler station. As a poet of the common things of life he stands alone, for he writes of practically nothing else. King Muḥammad Qulī Quṭb Shāh does indeed speak of everyday matters, but he also writes a good deal in a more conventional style. Saudā and Mīr have a few things that remind us of Naẓīr, and Inshā is very unconventional when he likes, but his subjects are far removed from Naẓīr's. To borrow an Urdu expression, Naẓīr 'can be compared only with himself.'

126. Naṣīr ud Dīn Shāh Naṣīr (d. 1838) belonged to Delhi and used to recite his poetry in Shāh 'Ālam's court. He twice visited Lucknow, first during the time of Muṣḥafī and Inshā, when he was received with great honour, second when Ātish and Nāsikh were at the height of their fame; this time his welcome was less effusive. Several times he went to Ḥaidarābād, where he became the head of a school of poetry. He was known for the splendour of his vocabulary and for the novelty and difficulty of his similes and metaphors. His fondness for old words is regarded by Indian critics as a bad fault. His work is generally rather insipid. He was the teacher of the famous poet, Żauq.

127. Shāh 'Ālam Āftāb, King of Delhi (1759–1806), was seized and blinded by the Rohilla chieftain, Ġulām Qādir, in 1788; his account of what he suffered at the hands of his enemies, in which naturally he expressed deep feeling, is the best of his writings. Another of his works is a romance called *Maẓmūn i Aqdas*. He also wrote a number of lyrics.

128. Niẓām ud Dīn Mamnūn (d. 1844) was in high favour with Akbar Shāh II of Delhi, in which city Mamnūn was born. He left a collection of poems consisting chiefly of lyrics, but containing also elegiac poems on the death of his relatives and friends, odes on religious subjects, and a few other poems. His reputation stood very high in his time.

IV

URDU POETRY IN LUCKNOW IN THE NINETEENTH CENTURY

WE have seen that owing to the troubles in Delhi nearly all the poets left for other places where they hoped to find greater peace, gain recognition for their talents and secure the means of livelihood. There were several courts where literary men were welcomed; chief among them were Ḥaidarābād, Patna and Lucknow. Of these Lucknow was the nearest—a matter of importance in those days of unrest and turmoil, when all journeys were dangerous. The Delhi poets were received with enthusiasm in Lucknow both by the court and by the populace; it soon became the centre of Urdu poetry. Life was luxurious and effeminate, particularly in the court, and the poets as court favourites came under its influence. Delhi and Lucknow differed in their literary point of view. Lucknow poetry reflected the court. It gave itself up to external things, such as outward ornament, rather than beauty of thought. It developed rules for language and idiom, restricted poetic licence and laid down laws for prosody and figures of speech, especially similes and metaphors. Vigour of style and depth of thought counted for little, verbal accuracy and idiomatic use of words were the ideal. Delhi was less careful about words and gave more attention to thought and subject. Many critics would subscribe to G̱ālib's dictum (which reminds us of a famous Italian saying) that the aim of a poet should be the 'thoughts of Delhi in the language of Lucknow.'

In the desire for power in the use of words Lucknow increased the length of the lyric (gazal) and the number of rhymes, till it became a mere string of words cleverly put together; and sometimes the poet's striving after colloquial speech led to his using the language of the gutter. Delhi on the other hand had suffered much; consequently it had more loftiness of imagination and vigour of thought. Lucknow used to be regarded by many Indians as feminine in its ways.

Elegies, or *marṣiyas* (see pp. 2, 34, 35), on the tragic events at Karbalā are characteristic of Muhammadan poetry, especially in Persia and India. They are essentially religious, indeed in the days before Ẓamīr and Khaliq, mentioned below, they were short devotional poems and little attention was paid to their literary quality. Ẓamīr changed that; and under Anīs and Dabīr the marṣiya became practically a form of epic, having however this limitation that it must always revolve round the death of Ḥasan, Ḥusain and the members of their family. Subject to this limitation, which is a very serious one, marṣiyas take in Urdu the place that epic poetry occupies in western lands. Apart from them Urdu has no epic poetry—a fact all the more remarkable when we remember the prominent place taken by epics in Hindi. These epics of Karbalā include historical narrative, moral and didactic teaching, description of natural scenery and delineation of human emotion. They suffer of course from their narrowness; every character is either friend or enemy, altogether good or entirely evil, and the only emotions are those which would be brought out by such a tragedy as that of Karbalā. Yet with all that, there is nothing so admirable in Urdu poetry as the marṣiya.

129. **Khaliq and Zamir.** MĪR MUSTAḤSAN KHALĪQ (1774–1804), one of the earliest elegiac writers in north India, was the son of the famous Mīr Ḥasan, and father of the still more famous Anīs. He began writing poetry at an early age. His father, not having time to instruct him, committed him to the care of Muṣḥafī. He made great progress, and on the occasion of a gathering of poets in his native place, Faiẓābād, read one of his lyrics with such effect that Ātish, who had come specially from Lucknow to grace the meeting, would not recite his own poem, saying there was no need for him when Khaliq was there.

His contemporary,

130. MUẒAFFAR ḤUSAIN ẒAMĪR, was another famous

writer of elegies. The two men constituted a pair who complemented each other, as has frequently happened in Urdu literature (p. 50). They were like Ātish and Nāsikh. Khaliq was simple and comparatively unlearned, but full of tenderness; Ẓamīr was learned and clever. To him belongs the credit of extending the scope of the elegy. Before his time elegies had been confined to descriptions of the events at Karbalā and had been intended as religious hymns of mourning, whereas now an elegy may extend to 1,000 lines and contain accounts of battles, individual heroes and their prowess, horses, accoutrements and natural scenery; or it may describe historical events with a view to increasing religious fervour. It is related that Ātish, on hearing an elegy composed by Dabīr, inquired 'Is this an elegy or an account of a wrestling match?' To-day such elegies are the rule and not the exception. It was Ẓamīr who led the way to this wider field.

Khaliq was a truer poet than Ẓamīr; he felt the grief he portrayed and spoke more to the heart; his language, too, was beautiful in its simplicity and correctness. Ẓamīr was more scholarly and more artificial; his language, though very good, was stilted and difficult to understand, and his fancies were far-fetched.

131. KARĀMAT 'ALĪ SHAHĪDĪ (d. 1840) was a native of Barelī, brought up in Lucknow, who lived at first a gay and careless life, but afterwards became a very religious man, went on pilgrimage, and died near Medina. It is remarkable that in a famous ode he had expressed a desire to die in Medina. Two of his books of poetry have been published, one containing odes, the other lyrics. He was a pupil of Muṣḥafī, and later of Shāh Naṣīr, and had special facility in writing poems in difficult metres.

132. DAYĀ SHAṄKAR KAUL NASĪM (1811–43) was a Kashmīrī paṇḍit who studied poetics under Ātish. His fame rests entirely on one poem, a romance called *Gulzār i Nasīm*, composed when he was 22. It greatly resembles Mīr Ḥasan's *Siḥr ul Bayān*, and is generally awarded the second place among Urdu poetic romances. Nasīm also translated *The Arabian Nights* into Urdū.

133 and 134. **Atish and Nasikh.** ḤAIDAR 'ALĪ ĀTISH

(d. 1846) and Imām Bakhsh Nāsikh (d. 1838). When Lucknow became the centre of Urdu poetry, these two important figures emerged to dominate literary circles till the death of Nāsikh in 1838, after which Ātish gave up writing. They corresponded to Saudā and Mīr of an earlier generation in Delhi. Ātish was the natural poet, Nāsikh the master of words. Ātish used simple, colloquial language, the language of everyday speech; his verses flow from his pen very naturally and reflect the dislike of luxurious court life which characterised the man himself. He was a good swordsman, a man of powerful physique, and much of his poetry is manly in tone; yet in many places he falls a victim to the prevailing fashion and describes merely the external attractions of the loved one's face or hair or hands. His enemies admitted his purity of language and correctness of idiom, but said that his verses were mere words with no power of imagination or poetical vigour. His friends, on the other hand, maintained that Nāsikh was bombastic and obscure, that his verses, largely plagiarised from Persian sources, were full of sound and fury, but devoid of poetry. They said also that he had with disastrous results failed to distinguished between odes and lyrics, and that when finally he tried to give up obscurity and wild imagination he became merely flabby.

Ātish is one of the best of Urdu lyric writers. He is the author of two collections of poems; the first compiled by himself contains not far short of 30,000 lines, the other, compiled by a pupil after his death, is less than a quarter of that length. His work is marked by uncomplaining pathos, true feeling, simple thoughts and correct language. Nāsikh, like Ātish, almost confined himself to lyrics; he left three volumes of poetry; the first, called *Daftar i Pareshān*, contains 18,000 lines, and the second nearly 30,000. The third is little esteemed. He wrote also a description of the birth of Muhammad, and a romance which is a translation of *Hadīs̤ i Mufassal*. He is characterised by vigorous and immoderate imagination, obscure language and turgid style.

Nāsikh was fond of Persian and Arabic words, and as far as possible avoided Hindi words. He was very careful about gender and laid down rules for it. Mīr, Saudā and the writers of their time allowed themselves great licence in matters of prosody, forms of words, length of syllables and archaic language. Nāsikh made strict rules and observed them. Before his time literary Urdu had been called rekhta and the name 'Urdū,' though found in Muṣḥafī and others was little used; now it became common. 'Rekhta' had also been employed to denote a lyrical poem; from this time onward it gave place to 'gazal,' a word which had been used, though rarely, by Saudā, Jur'at and Muṣḥafī. Some of the pupils of Nāsikh and Ātish hesitated about the excessive use of Arabic and Persian words, Persian constructions and Persian modes of erotic verse with its hyperboles, similes, metaphors and plays on words; their tendency was to avoid monotonous references to black tresses, moles on the face, doves, nightingales, drinking and taverns; and finally they turned back again to many Hindi words which had unwisely been given up.

135. Āgā Hajjū Sharf, a pupil of Ātish, exemplifies in an extreme form the movement mentioned above against Persian style. 'Abd us Salām and Ṣafīr Bilgrāmī have pointed out that he rejected the whole vocabulary of the wineshop.

As Ātish and Nāsikh remind us of Mīr and Saudā, so Sabā and Vazīr are a still fainter copy of the great originals.

136. Vazīr 'Alī Ṣabā (1795–1854) was a pupil of Ātish, while (136a) Muhammad Vazīr Vazīr (d. 1854) acknowledged Nāsikh as his master. Ṣabā left a large collection of lyrics called *Gunca e Ārzū*, in good idiomatic Urdu, but very artificial in thought. Vazīr's poems were collected immediately after his death; he was a very religious man and the greatest of the minor poets of his time. His work has been compared to a beautiful, but soulless body. It is all in one volume called *Daftar i Faṣāhat*. He was superior to Ṣabā in imagination and subject matter, but inferior in language and idiom.

137. Muḥammad Khān Rind (1797–1857) was born in Faiẓābād, where he lived till he was grown up, when he went to Lucknow. His first volumes of poems, written while he was still in Faiẓābād, were destroyed by him shortly after he arrived in Lucknow, and under the influence of

Ātish he wrote another to which he gave the name *Guldasta e 'Ishq*. In middle age he gave up his licentious mode of living and entered on the religious life. He was on his way to Mecca when he died. He cannot be called a great poet, but there was a certain amount of simple beauty in his writings.

138. 'ALĪ AUSAṮ RASHK (1799–1867), a pupil of Nāsikh, gave himself up almost entirely to improving the language and laying down rules for it. He was very fond of the colloquial, which he employed freely in his poems. He became a great authority on all points connected with idioms and use of words, but as a poet he was inferior. He died in the holy city of Karbalā. Two collections of his poems are extant, *Nagm i Mubārak* (1837) and *Nagm i Girāna* (1846). A third, said to be the best of all, has been lost. In 1840 he compiled an Urdu dictionary called *Nafs ul Lugāt*, part of which has been published.

139. MUHAMMAD RIẒA BARQ (d. 1857) was born in Lucknow. He attached himself to the court of Vājid 'Alī Shāh, who helped him in his career. He was fond of far-fetched metaphors and similes, delighted in puns, and wrote voluminously in the style of his teacher, Nāsikh. He followed his royal master into exile and wrote a rather uninspired account of his own loneliness.

140. ḤĀTIM 'ALĪ BEG MIHR (1814–79) is perhaps better known as a correspondent of Gālib than as a poet, for his own prolific writings do not display much poetic power. His chief collection of poems is called *Almās i Darakhshān*. He wrote several poetic romances, one of which, *Shu'ā e Mihr* (1858), won Gālib's admiration.

141. IMDĀD 'ALĪ BAḤR (1810–82) lived in poverty till he was an old man. He sat on a little mat every day and was visited by many people who smoked and discussed poetry. He and Vazīr and Rashk were Nāsikh's chief disciples. Rashk and he shared with their master a reputation for authoritative knowledge of Urdu. The Navāb of Rāmpūr, Kalb 'Alī Khān, summoned him to his court and gave him a salary which he enjoyed till homesickness made him return to poverty in Lucknow. His poems were collected by his friends. He is a second rate poet who combines verbal correctness with some facility of composition.

142. Dost 'Alī Khalīl (flor. 1860) was a great friend and faithful follower of Ātish. He was a writer of lyrics.

143. Ismā'īl Ḥusain Munīr (1819–81) lived a wandering life and wrote many poems. He wrote some good odes, a romance called *Ma'ārij ul Maẓāmīn*, and collections of poems which he called *Muntakhibāt i 'Ālam*, *Tanvīr ul Ash'ār* and *Nagm i Munīr*. He is typical of his time.

144. Mahdī Ḥasan Khān Ābād (flor. 1850) wrote a great deal of verse. His best known lyrics are those in *Nigāristān i 'Ishq*. He also compiled an anthology called *Bahāristān i Sukhan*.

All the Navābs of Lucknow wrote verse, but the most prolific was the last who reigned from 1847 to 1856 when he was banished to Calcutta. His name was

145. Vājid 'Alī Shāh Akhtar. Of his works, the best worth reading are perhaps his *Husn i Akhtar*, a poetic description of his exile, and the Letters which he wrote from Calcutta to his favourite wife in Lucknow. The British Museum possesses a valuable MS. of his unpublished poems.

146. Muẓaffar 'Alī Khān Asīr (1800–81) was another of Vājid 'Alī's courtiers. Apart from articles on grammar and prosody he wrote a complete work on prosody, several poetic romances and six other volumes of poetry. He had a considerable number of pupils, of whom the best known were Amīr Aḥmad Mīnāī and Aḥmad 'Alī Shauq (Nos. 178 and 238).

147. Arshad 'Alī Khān Qalaq (flor. 1850) is regarded by some as one of the greatest writers of romances (masnavīs). This opinion is based upon his *Ṭilism i Ulfat*, which is very popular, but has little merit beyond that of a clever use of words. He wrote also a well-known lyric on the Qaiṣar Bāg in Lucknow and some eulogiums of his master, Vājid 'Alī.

148. Mahdī 'Alī Khān Zakī (d. 1866) spent his life in wandering from one court to another. He wrote a book on rhyme and prosody entitled *Yād Gīr* (1848), and was the author of a short history of the Panjab (1850). The year of his death was probably 1866, not 1864 as sometimes stated. His poetic works, published in Lucknow, have not much value.

149. 'ALĪ KHĀN DARAKHSHĀN wrote moral and didactic poems in a good colloquial style with rather fanciful conceits. Along with Barq (No. 139) he accompanied Vājid 'Alī into exile.

150. ĀGĀ HASAN AMĀNAT (1815–58) was another of the second-rate poets of Lucknow. He wrote a number of elegies in honour of Ḥasan and Ḥusain, two collections of lyrics, and a very popular play called *Indar Sabhā*. Its special importance lies in the fact of its being the first drama in Urdu.

151. MUḤAMMAD ṢĀDIQ KHĀN AKHTAR (d. 1858) wrote in Persian at the court of Vājid 'Alī Shāh and left one volume of Urdu lyrics.

Anīs and Dabīr. 152. BABAR 'ALĪ ANĪS (1802–74) and No. 153, SALĀMAT 'ALĪ DABĪR (1803–75) are the two most famous elegy writers in Urdu. Elegiac epic poetry, the highest form of Urdu verse, reaches its culminating point in them. They are related to each other in the literary sphere as Mīr and Saudā had been a century before.

Anīs was the greater and more natural poet of the two. The considered literary judgment of to-day would probably say that he and Gālib and Mīr are the three greatest poets in the language. Poetry seems to be hereditary in his family. His great-grandfather Ẓāḥik, his grandfather Mīr Ḥasan, his father Khaliq, were all poets, and the gift has been given also to his son Nafīs, his brother Mūnis, his grandson Jalīs, and his great-grandson 'Ārif. He himself is the greatest of all, his grandfather comes next, and his brother Mūnis third. He employed an enormous number of words, but preferred a simple, easy and flowing style. His family is famous for the use of pure and idiomatic Urdu. He had a wonderful power of description. This is seen best when he depicts human feelings, especially pathos and bravery, or scenes of nature and fighting. He writes as if he had been present himself on the occasions which he describes and as if the people had spoken the very words which he has put down. His works have been published in four volumes containing more than a hundred elegies with well over 100,000 lines. A good idea of his writing may be obtained from *Vāqi'āt i Karbalā*, a volume of selections so connected as to make a single story. It contains between 5,000 and 6,000 lines.

Dabīr showed more scholarship in his poetry than Anīs, and in power of imagination was his superior; but his style was sometimes laboured, and he tended to use unsuitable or great swelling words which lack the vividness of an eyewitness. He wrote approximately half as much as Anīs; like Anīs he confined himself to elegies. His works have been published in two large volumes. He too had a very extensive vocabulary; his ideas were sometimes fanciful and clever rather than impressive, and his pathos was much less true to life than the real sorrow depicted in the verses of Anīs.

154. Mīr Muḥammad Navāb Mūnis (d. 1875) was the brother of the famous Anīs, and son of the elegy writer Khaliq. Some have maintained that he was as good a poet as his brother. He had a great command over language which he showed in his elegies. At first he wrote ordinary lyrics, but latterly confined himself to elegies, by which alone he is known. He was a very religious man, and apart from his frequent appearances to read elegies, he was little seen. His powers of recitation were far-famed. His works are published in two volumes of considerable size. His brother's death in 1874 was a severe blow to him, and he himself died very suddenly in the following year. Being childless he had adopted his sister's son.

155. Navāb Mirzā Shauq (d. 1871) was a pupil of Ātish, famed for his masnavis or romantic love stories, four in number—*Bahār i 'Ishq*, *Zahr i 'Ishq*, *Lazzat i 'Ishq*, and *Fareb i 'Ishq*. They enjoyed considerable popularity in Lucknow and the author was regarded as one of the best masnavi writers in the language, but if the truth be told their chief merits are idiomatic use of good Urdu and an excellent choice of rhymes. They are valueless as stories, and the conversations are stilted. His *Lazzat i 'Ishq* is not unlike Mīr Ḥasan's *Siḥr ul Bayān*. His *Bahār i 'Ishq* is founded upon Asar's *Khwāb o Khayāl* and shows the influence of that poem in both language and style, the similarity amounting sometimes to actual plagiarism.

156. Sayyid Mirzā Ta'ashshuq (d. 1891) brother of

Husain Mirzā 'Ishq, and son of Mīr Uns, was noted for his elegies. His lyrics were poor, but after writing a few he took to elegies and surpassed all others of his time in the pathos which he infused into them. His words were well chosen and his ideas striking. His published works comprise two volumes of elegies and forty pages of love lyrics, 55 in number.

157. Husain Mirzā 'Ishq (d. before 1890), elder brother of the foregoing was, like him, an elegy writer of considerable ability, but not so popular. His elegies were published in two volumes.

158. Khurshīd 'Alī Nafīs (1819–1901) was the son of Anīs and nephew of Mūnis, and followed the tradition which they had laid down. He wrote a great deal, but only one small volume has been published. Even in advanced age he used to hold enthralled the audiences which went to hear him recite.

159. Mustafā Mirzā Rashīd (1845–1917), generally called Piyāre Sāhib, was the son-in-law of Anīs and nephew of Ta'ashshuq and 'Ishq. He followed his uncles rather than his more talented father-in-law. Unlike most elegy writers he wrote many love lyrics; they have no merit beyond that of elegance. His elegies are much better. He is said to write in the 'Spring Style,' i.e. he brings into his elegies descriptions of Spring.

160. 'Alī Muhammad 'Ārif (1861–1916), great-grandson of Anīs, first wrote lyrics, but became afterwards a well-known elegy writer. He was brought up by his grandfather, Nafīs, whom he greatly resembled in character and poetic style.

V

THE SECOND DELHI PERIOD AND THE FOUR POETS OF RAMPUR

A. THE SECOND DELHI PERIOD

We have seen how poetry declined in Delhi. It never entirely ceased and a few poets were always to be found who kept the flame alive. In the second quarter of the nineteenth century there was a revival of poetry associated with the names of Mūmin, Zauq and Gālib. The last King of Delhi, Bahādur Shāh, was himself a poet and encouraged the poets at his court. He was exiled to Burma immediately after the Mutiny and died in 1862.

161. **Zauq.** Muhammad Ibrahīm Zauq (1789–1854) was the first poet of importance after the revival of literature in Delhi. Most of his writings were lost in the Mutiny, but Āzād and other pupils collected what they could, and now we have about 12,000 lines which give a good idea of his work. He was the son of a poor man, a servant in Delhi, and he remained poor till quite late in life. Like his teacher, Naṣir, with whom he afterwards quarrelled, he belonged in poetic method to Lucknow rather than to Delhi, and shows considerable resemblance to Nāsikh. He had the same tendency to over-rate the value of mere words and idioms, and the same fondness for playing with meanings. This undoubtedly lessened his poetic power. At the same time he was certainly one of the greatest ode writers in Urdu; some critics would rank him first. He has left fifteen odes of an average length of about 250 lines each. He wrote also numerous lyrics, but not with the same success.

He had many pupils; the most famous of them was Āzād, who cherished his memory with great affection and wrote an account of his life as well as publishing his poems. Another of his pupils was Bahādur Shāh II (No. 164), whose verses he used to correct. Zauq's power of expression was greater than his poetic feeling, but he wrote with a great sense of harmony and considerable vigour.

162. **Galib.** Asad Ullāh Khān Gālib (1797–1869) stands in the front rank of Urdu poets; one enthusiast has said that India possesses two inspired books—the Vedas and the poems of Gālib. Without going so far as that, most will agree that he is one of the first three Urdu poets. He was married when a mere boy and shortly after his marriage fell in with a Persian named Hormuzd, a Pārsī who had embraced Islām. Gālib took him in and for two years studied Persian with him, thus laying the foundation of his profound knowledge of the language. He wrote more in Persian than in Urdu; in fact for many years he despised Urdu, and when he began using it as a literary medium, it was only to show that he could do so as well as others. But gradually the fascination of the language laid hold upon him and he became very proud of his proficiency in it. For a time his Urdu poetry was impregnated with Persian, but it was criticised by his friends and parodied by others. In the end he destroyed much of his over-Persianised composition and wrote in a much simpler and purer style.

Most previous poets were confined to a narrow circle of ideas. Gālib not only struck out new lines of thought, but adopted notable methods of treatment. He was a man of great ability, a deep thinker, somewhat careless in matters of religion, full of humour, but mixing humorous and serious subjects in a very attractive way. He could handle verse and prose with equal facility. His best known works are his Urdu poems (a collection of not more than three or four thousand lines) and two volumes of prose (see No. 208). One of these, *'Ud ī Hindī*, contains letters and reviews, the other, *Urdū e Mu'allā*, letters only. When we read his letters we feel as if the man were sitting opposite to us talking to us in his inimitable way. His reviews are in a very different style. In writing appreciations of his friends' books, he yielded to the custom of the time and employed the measured rhythmic prose which was regarded as necessary. These reviews will be forgotten when people still read with delight the letters in which he speaks so naturally of his everyday joys and sorrows, chiefly sorrows, alas! for he had indifferent health, none of his children survived, and he suffered much from the buffetings of fortune.

He was always improving his style. First he followed artificial Persian writers, and then Nāsikh who was less artificial, but the poems of his later years show that he was then following Mīr in the expression of yearning and pathos, sometimes even in simplicity of language. He was particularly successful as a writer of lyrics.

163. Muḥammad Mūmin Khān Mūmin (1800–51), one of the three important Delhi poets in the time of Bahādur Shāh II, was fond of astrology and medicine as well as poetry. His reputation stands higher now than ever before, and he is looked upon as a very good poet, though not in the first rank. He wrote many lyrics, nine odes, the best of which is that addressed to the Navāb of Ṭonk in recognition of help received, several erotic romances, and some good masnavīs of an autobiographical nature. One poem, called *Masnavī e Jihādiya*, was a warlike poem against the Sikhs. His love of Persian constructions makes him obscure. His first master, the poet Shāh Naṣīr, though a native of Delhi, had a great deal of the Lucknow manner; and Mūmin too was given to fanciful ideas and difficult images.

164. Bahādur Shāh II, Ẓafar (1775–1862), King of Delhi (1837–58), was the author of several volumes of verse, mostly lyrics, over 130,000 lines in all. It has been said that he was a better poet than king, but even his writings show more skill in weaving a web of words than true poetry. He composed with great ease, and some of his writings have attained considerable popularity. On well worn themes he wrote with machine-like regularity, but he failed when he tried new subjects. Some critics unkindly ascribe much of his work to his poetical teacher, Ẕauq, but probably the great majority of it is his own.

165. Aṣgar ʿAlī Khān Nasīm of Delhi (1794–1864), not to be confounded with Dayā Shankar Kaul Nasīm, the author of *Gulzār i Nasīm*, left Delhi for Lucknow, where he became known as a prolific writer and had many pupils. Muḥsin ʿAlī Mūsavī, in his anthology, *Sarāpā Sukhan*

(1852), in which he quotes from no less than 700 authors, mostly contemporary, gives great praise to Nasim for his ability as an instructor of poetics. That he deserved this praise is evidenced by the fact that, though a Delhi man writing in the Delhi style, he was highly esteemed by a large band of pupils in Lucknow. He was a remarkable poet who combined happy thoughts with a bright style and effective language. He was at his best in his introductions to the sections of *The Arabian Nights.* These have been declared superior to the work of the Persian poet Ẓuhūrī.

166. Mīr Ḥusain Taskīn (1803–51) was born in Delhi and studied poetry under Shāh Naṣir till the latter's death in 1838, when he enrolled himself under the disciples of Mūmin. He had some difficulty in gaining a livelihood, but finally settled in Rāmpūr where he died. No collection of his poems is extant, but from extracts in anthologies, his verses, and especially his lyrics, are seen to be written in an attractive style.

167. Muṣṭafā Khān Sheftā (1806–69) was a very religious man born and brought up in Delhi, who in later life performed the pilgrimage to Mecca. There are collections of his poems in both Urdu and Persian, but he is best known by his biographical anthology of Urdu poets, *Gulshan i Bekhār.*

168. Sadr ud Dīn Khān Āzurda (1789–1868) was a Kashmiri with a great reputation for learning in Arabic and Persian. He was a Government official held in great respect by a large circle of friends and pupils. In spite of his learning he wrote in an extremely simple manner. He compiled an anthology and wrote a considerable amount of verse; but as nothing has been published we have to judge of his ability by stray quotations.

169. Qurbān 'Alī Sālik (d. 1875) was born in Ḥaidarābād, went to Delhi at the age of six, and was brought up there. He wrote a powerful elegy on the death of his brother. One collection of his poems is called *Hanjār i Sālik*; another, compiled by his son who died about ten years ago, was published under the name of *Maikhāna e Sālik.* He owed most of his instruction to Gālib (No. 162).

He is noted for the purity of his style, which sometimes rises to eloquence, and for the pathos of some of his love passages. In late life he returned to Ḥaidarābād where he died. He had a vivid imagination and was good at thinking out new methods of expression.

170. Ẓiyā ud Dīn Rakhshān (d. 1883) was a relative and pupil of Ġālib. His MSS. are still in the hands of his son, Aḥmad Sa'id Khān Ṭālib (b. 1852), who is also a poet; but they have not yet been published.

171. Shahāb ud Dīn Sāqib (1840–69), son of Rakhshān and elder brother of Ṭālib, was a poet of considerable merit. He had two sons who are still alive and write poetry. The elder, No. 172, Shujā' ud Dīn Tābān, though he has written a good deal, is not well known. The other, Sirāj ud Dīn Sāil (No. 173), has a great reputation in Delhi at the present time.

174. Muḥammad Zakariya Khān Zakī (1839–1903) was an inspector of schools in the United Provinces. He was born in Delhi and looked to Ġālib as his teacher; more than any other of Ġālib's pupils he wrote in the style of the master, but he had only slight success. He was fond of new subjects, but when a subject did not appeal to him, he had the good sense to avoid it. His thoughts were fresh and his style pleasing. One volume of poems was published during his lifetime; sufficient material to fill another is still in the hands of his friends.

175. Ẓahīr ud Dīn Ẓahīr (born c. 1835, d. 1911) spent his life in different Indian States, and like Sālik, died in Ḥaidarābād. Though he was a pupil of Ẕauq he wrote more like Mūmin and Dāġ; sometimes his style was forceful, but often he indulged in merely fanciful ideas. He left several collections of poems, but only one, *Gulistān i Sukhan*, has been printed.

176. Umrāo Mirzā Anvar (c. 1840–78), younger brother of Ẓahīr, had a gift of effective language and a polished style which was greatly admired during his lifetime; so much so that in the poetic assemblies of Delhi held in the late fifties of the last century, and attended by the greater poets of the time, not a few gave Anvar preference over the others. He was a clever writer rather than a great poet.

His friends held that he was a mixture of Mūmin, Gālib and Zauq. He passed his later years amid many anxieties and died young. Most of his work was lost, but some, about an eighth of the whole, was collected and published after his death. He is remembered specially for his treatment of love themes.

177. Mīr Mahdī Majrūḥ (d. 1902) is known to us chiefly by the fact that in Gālib's *'Ūd i Hindī* there are many letters addressed to him showing the affection which the author bore him. In 1898 Majrūḥ published a volume of poetry called *Maẓhar i Ma'ānī* in which may be traced a gentle, if commonplace, simplicity of thought.

B. THE FOUR POETS AT THE RĀMPŪR COURT

178. **Amīr and Dāg.** In Amīr Aḥmad Mīnāī (1828–1900) and No. 179, Navāb Mirzā Khān Dāg (1831–1905) we have once more an example of a pair of poets (p. 50). Much of what has been said of Saudā and Mīr might be said of Amīr and Dāg. They along with Taslīm and Jalāl, were the chief ornaments of the court of Rāmpūr after the Mutiny had led to the breaking up of the court in Lucknow. Amīr was the scholarly man, the master of high sounding words, and Dāg the natural poet with a greater flow of simple idiomatic language. Like Saudā, Amīr was superior in odes which demand splendour of style, while Dāg, like Mīr, excelled in love lyrics where simplicity and pathos are more necessary. Unfortunately both of them, but especially Dāg, indulged in verse of inferior moral tone. Amīr's scholarship is attested by his dictionary *Amīr ul Lugāt*. This was begun on a grandiose scale, but only two parts were published, and the dictionary came to an end with the first letter still incomplete. He wrote a great many poems on religious subjects, especially dealing with the birth, life, death and character of Muḥammad. They are not, however, very successful; the true poetic fire is wanting, and to the devout Muslim they appear cold and formal. His first collection of lyrics was lost in the upheavals of 1857; and consequently the second, *Mir'āt ul Gāib*, is usually called his first. After he had written it he felt that the day for that kind of verse was over; he realised

that his friendly rival Dāg was getting the public ear better than he, and determined to alter his style, a difficult thing for a man of his age to do. But it used to be said of him that the older he got the younger he grew. In copying Dāg he became simpler and employed more everyday idioms. Some critics consider his second collection, *Ṣanamkhāna e 'Ishq*, superior to his first, but it is generally agreed that he failed to equal Dāg. This is not to be wondered at, especially as Dāg was a master of short lyrics. His third collection was entirely given up to praise of Muhammad (a species of verse called *na't*). Mention must also be made of his valuable volume of *Letters* the publication of which was suggested by the appearance of Gālib's *Letters*. His anthology *Intikhāb i Yādgār* (1873) gives biographical details of poets who had lived in Rāmpūr. He spent many years in that city and then left it for Ḥaidarābād, where he died shortly after his arrival. (See No. 214.)

Dāg ranks very high in the estimation of his literary fellow-countrymen, most of whom would place him in the first twelve Urdu poets. He writes with great fluency in simple and beautiful language, and is a perfect 'river of correct idioms,' but he fails to sound real depths of feeling. He lived on into the twentieth century, but he is a writer of the old school, a pupil of Zauq who inclined to the Lucknow manner, even though he belonged to Delhi. Dāg's work falls into two periods, the Rāmpūr period and the Ḥaidarābād period. So long as he lived in Rāmpūr he was surrounded by other poets whose criticism stimulated him to do his best, and there he produced his best work—*Gulzār i Dāg*, *Āftāb i Dāg* and *Faryād i Dāg*. After he went to Haidarābād he wrote *Mahtāb i Dāg* and *Yādgār i Dāg* with its supplement. Here he lived a life of ease, fêted on every side with no one to criticise his work. He grew careless and his poetry suffered. He is considered one of the great lyrists, but it is not easy to be enthusiastic about him.

180. Taslīm (1820–1911). His real name was Aḥmad Ḥusain, but he was always known by the name Amīr Ullāh. Not long after his birth near Faiẓābād his family removed to Lucknow where he spent much of his life in

search of a livelihood, for he was always poor. He belonged essentially to the old-fashioned way of thinking and his verses do not appeal much to us now. He wrote eight romances (of which the most esteemed are *Nāla e Taslīm*, *Ṣubaḥ i Khandā* and *Dil o Jān*), *Safarnama e Navāb i Rāmpūr* (not published), a long drawn out account of the travels of the Navāb of Rāmpūr, about 50,000 lines in length, and five other collections of poetry, of which one is in MS., one was lost in the Mutiny, and three have been published under the titles of *Nazm i Arjmand*, *Nazm i Dilafroz*, and *Daftar i Khayāl*.

Nazm i Dilafroz contains, approximately, 2,000 lines of laudatory odes, about 11,000 lines of lyrics and 1,300 lines of other kinds of poetry. The *Daftar i Khayāl* is a volume about half the size of that just mentioned and has nothing but short lyrics. *Nazm i Arjmand* is his best collection of lyrics. His odes are in a rather simple style like that considered appropriate to lyrics. Among the poets assembled in Rāmpūr he was the best romance writer; his language was simple and solemn with much power of imagination. He had many pupils of whom the best are Hasrat Mohānī, the well-known public speaker.

181. ẒĀMIN ʿALĪ JALĀL (1834–1909) was famous in the court of Rāmpūr for his interest in matters relating to grammar and prosody. In addition to four volumes of perhaps 20,000 lines in all, containing odes and lyrics, he wrote several books on language. Some of them are very short, under 100 pages. One called *Mufīd ush Shuʿarā* is a guide to the gender of words; another, much longer, *Sarmāya e Zabān i Urdū*, is a useful collection of idioms. In *Qawāʿid ul Muntakhab* he discusses changes in words. He compiled also a couple of Urdu dictionaries.

It is a little difficult to understand upon what the fame of men like Taslīm and Jalāl rests. Their odes and lyrics are conventional; their merit is clever expression more than deep feeling. The lyrics contain the usual complaints against the hard-hearted, murderous loved one, and describe the torments of the lover with the scars on his heart; the odes are fulsome panegyrics. The new age of Urdu poetry had not yet come for them.

VI

URDU PROSE

A. EARLY PROSE WRITERS

We noticed above (pp. 18–20, 24) that some of the earliest literature in the Deccan was religious prose. 'Ain ud Din (Ganj ul 'Ilm; d. 1393); Khājā Banda Navāz (d. 1422), author of *Mi'rāj ul 'Āshiqīn* and *Hidāyat Nāma*; Shāh Mīrān Jī, author of *Jal Tarang* (d. 1496); his son Shāh Burhān, (d. 1582), author of *Kalimat ul Haqāiq* and other prose works, were the most important. It must not be forgotten that none of these works were literary in the strict sense of the term; they were purely religious in character. Still the fact remains that they were prose, and some of them good prose. Thus we have as early as the end of the fourteenth century Urdu or Dakhnī prose which is not nearly so far from the Urdu of to-day as the English of Piers Plowman is from modern English. Perhaps a comparison with Chaucer would express the difference better.

In the seventeenth century were written *Miftāḥ ul Khairāt* (about 1630); *Sab Ras*, a Ṣūfī religious work by Vajhī (1634); 'Abdullāh's *Aḥkām uṣ Ṣalawāt* (1662); Valī Ullāh Qādrī's *Ma'rifat us Sulūk* (1688); and Shāh Muḥammad Qādrī's tracts of about the same date, all of which have already been mentioned. The Deccan did not produce much literary prose.

182. Mīr Ja'far Zaṭallī (c. 1659–1713; No. 94). In extant MSS. of his work may be found examples of Urdu prose sufficient in amount to fill about two pages. They are disconnected sentences, but are smooth and natural; evidently they represent his ordinary speech.

183. A prose work often heard of is Faẓlī's *Dah Majlis*, translated from the Persian *Rauẓat ush Shuhadā*, with a

preface, also in Urdu prose, stating how he came to do the translation. It is referred to in Āzād's *Āb i Ḥayāt* and a quotation from it is given, but no MS. is known to exist and nothing further has been discovered about it.

183a. MUḤAMMAD ḤUSAIN KALĪM, as we have seen (No. 105), wrote prose as well as verse. Some have doubted his having written prose. Garcin de Tassy takes certain Persian words from Mīr Hasan's anthology to mean 'he wrote a treatise on the spread of Hindi,' but the word translated 'spread' should be read as an almost identical word meaning 'prose.' The passage is then clearly seen to state that Kalīm wrote Hindī prose (Hindī meaning Urdu); further, Mīr Hasan's illustrative quotation is prose. It refers to the Emperor Aḥmad Shāh as blind, which suggests 1754, or shortly after, as the date.

184. The poet SAUDĀ (No. 103) translated into Urdu verse Mīr's romance *Shu'la e 'Ishq*; this translation is not now extant, but a few lines of the Urdu preface to his own poems may still be read. It is astonishing how clumsy and stilted both Saudā and Faẓlī are. Their prose suggests the early efforts of people imperfectly acquainted with a language. It is full of awkward Persian constructions and rhythmical jingle. Since they were writing their native language, the explanation must be that they felt bound to reject straightforward conversational Urdu in favour of Persianised, semi-poetical composition. Zaṭalli's sentences, though about 30 years earlier, are much superior.

185. MUḤAMMAD 'AṬĀ ḤUSAIN TAḤSĪN of Iṭāvā (Etawa) is the author of *Nau Ṭarz i Muraṣṣa'*, usually said to be a translation of *Cahār Darvesh* attributed to Amīr Khusrau, but entirely unknown. (See No. 188.) No such work appears in the list of Khusrau's writings. *Nau Ṭarz i Muraṣṣa'* is important, but it has never been popular; it has too many Persian and Arabic words in it, and is now hardly ever heard of. Recent researches go to show that it was composed about 1770, nearly 30 years earlier than usually stated.

B. THE FORT WILLIAM TRANSLATORS

DR. J. B. GILCHRIST and FORT WILLIAM COLLEGE, CALCUTTA. The year 1800 is important in the history of Urdu. In that year Fort William College, Calcutta, was founded by the East India Company for the instruction of its servants in Indian languages, and at its head was placed an Edinburgh medical man, Dr. J. B. Gilchrist. Though he was compelled by ill-health to resign in 1804, he had already appointed a band of Indian scholars, both Hindu and Muḥammadan, to do translation and other literary work. Sanskrit books were translated into Hindi (Khaṛi Boli), and Arabic or Persian into Urdu. In this way he had given a great impetus to prose composition in these languages. It is true that after Gilchrist left the country the movement hung fire, but it is not possible to doubt that the revival of interest which took place later on was in great measure due to his work.

The names which follow (Nos. 186 to 198) were all associated with Fort William.

186. MIRZĀ 'ALĪ LUṬF was a poet of little merit, but famous for his biographical anthology named *Gulshan i Hind*, a translation from Persian. He tells us in the preface that it was written and compiled at Dr. Gilchrist's request. This is a valuable work in simple and good Urdu, giving much information about poets and society at that time. The language shows many traces of Dakhnī influence, for Luṭf was living in the Deccan when asked to write the book. It is in two parts, the first of 400 pages contains notices of sixty 'good' poets, while the second part is devoted to poets of inferior rank.

187. SAYYID ḤAIDAR BAKHSH ḤAIDARĪ, of Delhi, who died in 1828, translated many works from Persian into Urdu. He entered Dr. Gilchrist's service in 1801. His best-known works are the following: *Ārāish i Maḥfil* (1801), an adaptation of the story of Ḥātim Ṭāī; *Toṭā Kahānī*, (1801) translated from the *Ṭūṭīnāma* of Muhammad Qādrī: less important translations are *Gulzār i Dānish* from 'Ināyat Ullāh's *Bahār i Dānish*, *Gul i Magfirat* from the *Rauẓat ush Shuhadā* of Ḥusain Vā'iẓ Kāshifī, and *Tārīkh i Nādirī* from Mirzā Muḥammad Mahdī's history of the Emperor Nādir

Shāh. Still earlier than these is *Qiṣṣa e Lailā o Majnūn*. He also wrote a little verse. The language is good and idiomatic, remarkably like modern Urdu, and there is little difficulty in reading it.

188. MĪR AMMAN of Delhi in 1801 wrote *Bāg̱ o Bahār*, which he professed to have translated from 'Amīr Khusrau's *Cahār Darvesh*,' but almost certainly Khusrau never wrote such a work. The *Bāg̱ o Bahār* is perhaps a re-telling of Taḥsīn's *Nau Ṭarz i Muraṣṣa'* mentioned above (No. 185), which it has superseded in popular favour. Mīr Amman in his preface gave an account of the origin of the Urdu language; this is responsible for the erroneous views which for long prevailed and have not been wholly given up yet. In 1806 he translated Ḥusain Vā'iẓ Kāshifī's *Akhlāq i Muḥsinī*, to which he gave the name of *Ganj i Khūbī*. It is a book of 366 pages. His style is perhaps better than that of any other of Gilchrist's helpers; it drew forth a special encomium from Sir Sayyid Aḥmad. Mīr Amman's style in prose may be said to correspond to Mīr Taqī's in poetry.

189. BAHĀDUR 'ALĪ ḤUSAINĪ in 1802 told in prose the story of Mīr Ḥasan's romance *Siḥr ul Bayān*, giving it the name of *Naṡr i Benaẓīr*. His other works are: *Akhlāq i Hindī* (1802), a translation of a Persian version of the Sanskrit *Hitopadeśa*; *Tarjuma e Tārīkh i Āsām* (1805) from the Persian of Valī Aḥmad Shahab ud Dīn; a little pamphlet on Urdu grammar with various titles, apparently adapted from some Grammar by Gilchrist. He assisted also in the *Oriental Fabulist*, a translation of some of *Æsop's Fables* and in a translation of the *Qur'ān*.

190. SHER 'ALĪ AFSOS of Delhi is best known for his *Arāish i Maḥfil*, which, though based upon the Persian *Khulāṣat ut Tavārīkh* of Sujān Rāe of Paṭeāla, is practically an original work, and one of considerable ability; in addition to this he revised Nihāl Cand's *Maẕhab i 'Ishq*, Bahādur 'Alī Ḥusainī's *Naṡr i Benaẓīr*, and Muhammad Ismā'īl's *Bahār i Dānish*; finally he translated the *Gulistān* of Sa'dī into Urdu with the name of *Bāg̱ i Urdū*.

191. ḤAFĪẒ UD DĪN AḤMAD of Delhi in 1803 translated Abu'l Faẓl's *'Ayār i Dānish* calling it *Khirad Afroz*.

192. Nihāl Cand Lāhaurī translated *Maẕhab i 'Ishq* (1802) from a Persian version of the Hindi *Gul i Bakāvalī*, a story reproduced in verse by Dayā Shankar Kaul Nasīm in his famous romance, *Gulzār i Nasīm*. Nihāl Cand was born in Delhi, but left it to live in Lahore, on account of which he is known as 'Lāhaurī.' He calls the Urdu of his translation 'Hindī rekhta.' In the catalogue of the Asiatic Society of Bengal the next entry after Nihāl Cand's work is '*aiẓan manẓūm*,' i.e. 'the same in verse,' but this is probably by another hand.

193. Lāllū Lāl is more famous for his work in Hindi, both Khaṛī Bolī and Braj, but along with Kāẓim 'Alī Javān he translated into Urdu, or Urdu and Khaṛī Bolī mixed, *Singhāsan Battīsī* and *Śakuntalā*; he also helped Maẓhar 'Alī Vilā with *Baitāl Pacīsī* and *Mādhunal* (1805). In 1810 he compiled *Laṭāif i Hindī*, partly Urdu and partly Hindi.

194. Kāẓim 'Alī Javān in 1802 translated *Śakuntalā* into Urdu with the aid of Lallū Lāl whom he helped with the translation of *Singhāsan Battīsī*. His *Dastūr i Hind* is a poetical account of the months of the year with the feasts that occur in each.

195. Maẓhar 'Alī Vilā, apart from a large volume of mediocre poetry, and the works in which Lallū Lāl helped him as mentioned above, produced the following translations: *At Pandnāma* said to be from Sa'dī, *Tārīkh i Sher Shāhī*, *Haft Gulshan*, *Jahāngīr Shāhī*, and under the guidance of Dr. Gilchrist a little textbook, *Atālīq i Hindī*.

196. Ikrām 'Alī made from a famous Arabic work a translation which has been greatly praised. It bears the name of the original, *Ikhvān uṣ Ṣafā*. The Urdu is on the whole extremely good. The work was finished in 1810.

197. Amānat Ullāh Shaidā translated *Akhlāq i Jalālī* (1804), and *Hidāyat ul Islām* (1804) which is partly in Arabic. He wrote also a little Urdu grammar in Urdu verse.

198. Benī Nārāyan is the author of *Dīvān i Jahān*, a bibliographical anthology of Urdu poets (1814). Three years earlier he translated a Persian book under the name of *Cār Gulshan*. He is credited also with a little book of stories, *Qiṣṣajāt*, and a translation from the Persian, *Tanbīh ul Ġāfilīn*. These are much later than the others.

C. URDU PROSE WRITERS OF THE NINETEENTH CENTURY

The Fort William writers were chiefly translators; before passing on to Urdu literary prose, we may mention a group of three whose works were religious rather than literary.

199. Maulvī Ismā'īl, the reformer (1796–1831), was the author of *Taqviyyat ul Imān* and a number of tracts. He was killed during a religious war with the Sikhs. An English translation of the first part of *Taqviyyat ul Imān* was printed in the *Journal of the Royal Asiatic Society*, XIII, 316 ff.

200. Shāh Rafī' ud Dīn (1749–1818) and No. 201, Shāh 'Abd ul Qādir (1753–1815) were the sons of the famous Shāh Valī Ullāh, who translated the Qur'ān into Persian in 1737. These two brothers were learned and religious men. Each of them made a translation of the Qur'ān into Urdu; that of the younger brother (1790) is much better known. It has been greatly praised by Naẕīr Aḥmad, who himself about a century later made an Urdu translation of the Qur'ān (No. 221).

202. Khalīl Ullāh Khān Ashk of Faiẕābād produced a number of works, both original and translations. They are *Muntakhab ul Favaid* (1799, translated from Persian); *Qiṣṣa e Amīr Hamza* (1800, original); *Gulzār i Cīn* (1804), an original prose romance; *Intikhāb i Sulṭāniya* (1804), a short original history of the kings of Delhi; *Vāqi'āt i Akbarī* (1809) a translation of Abu'l Faẕl's *Akbar Nāma* and the same author's *Tārīkh i Akbarī*; lastly a short treatise on Physics, *Risāla e Kāīnāt*.

203. Mirzā Jān Ṭaish produced some verse which has been published, and a little book on Urdu idioms.

204. Inshā Allāh Khān Inshā (d. 1817) has been described under the poets of Delhi. He did not write Urdu prose, but in *Daryā e Laṭāfat* (1807) he gives several examples of Urdu letters and conversations which are remarkable for the close resemblance to everyday Urdu to-day. They are a tribute to his versatility. (See p. 55.)

205. Sa'ādat Yār Khān Rangīn (1756–1834) and his poetical works have been dealt with (p. 56) and his two

Urdu prose works have also been mentioned. He wrote in a fluent and easy style.

206. Faqīr Ullāh Goyā (d. between 1845 and 1850) was the author of *Bostān i Ḥikmat*, a prose translation of the *Anvār i Suhailī* (1835). He also wrote verse.

207. Rajab ʿAlī Beg Surūr (d. 1867) is famous as the ablest author of the old rhythmical prose based on Persian models. He was brought up in Lucknow, a place for which he ever retained a great affection. His best-known work is the fanciful story, *Fasāna e ʿAjāib*. The date is quite uncertain. His *Shabistān i Surūr* contains stories from *The Arabian Nights*. Other tales composed by him are *Shigūfa e Muḥabbat* (1851) and *Sharr i ʿIshq*. He also translated from Persian, *Surūr i Sulṭānī* and *Gulzār i Surūr*. He published a collection of letters, *Inshā e Surūr*, useful specimens of a now obsolete style, and wrote an ode on the marriage of the Prince of Wales, afterwards King Edward VII. His writings are valuable as describing life and society in Lucknow 100 years ago, and as the best examples of rhythmical Urdu, but they do not appeal to us now, for his pictures of Lucknow life are like a far-off fairy tale, and the style is florid and artificial. It is not met with in these days.

208. Asad Ullāh K͟hān G͟ālib has been spoken of already (No. 162). The fascination of his letters lies in their naturalness. He changed the whole course of Urdu letter-writing, substituting the natural for the artificial. Many authors have since then published letters, but G͟ālib's have never been equalled. Apart from *ʿŪd i Hindī* and *Urdū e Muʿallā* he has not written much Urdu prose of importance. He is the author of a few pamphlets and part of a novel. His reviews, found in *ʿŪd i Hindī* along with letters, are in the formal style which the time demanded. His preface to Mīr Lāl's *Sirāj ul Maʿrifat* is a very good example of this style.

209. G͟hulām Imām Shahīd was a contemporary writer the date of whose birth and death is not known. He wrote both prose and poetry in a flowery style. He was a religious teacher with many pupils, and because of his writings in praise of Muḥammad, was called Maddāḥ i Nabī (Praiser of the Prophet), and ʿĀshiq i Rasūl (Lover of the Apostle). His

works include *Inshā e Bahār i Bekhazān* (1866), verses on the birth of Muhammad called *Majmū'a e Maulūd i Sharīf*, and some other poems, chiefly odes and love lyrics.

210. RĀM CANDAR wrote principally about higher mathematics and allied subjects, on which he published nine volumes. He was converted to Christianity in 1852 and baptised the following year. His literary works were *Kitāb i 'Ajāib i Rozgār* on the marvels of the age, and *Tazkirat ul Kāmilīn* (1849), an account in 200 pages of the lives of famous men.

211. 'ABD UL KARĪM in 1845 translated *The Arabian Nights* for the use of schools. The Urdu is simple and good, being free from all superfluous ornament.

212. **Sayyid Ahmad.** SIR SAYYID AHMAD (1817–98) exercised more influence upon Urdu than perhaps any other single man in the nineteenth century. He occupied many positions under the Government, wrote many books, started magazines, and helped to found societies, doing much to increase friendly feelings between Europeans and Indians. In 1847 he completed *Āṣār us Sanādīd*, on the important buildings in Delhi, and in the following year began his history of Bijnaur. He was the author of many tracts on religious subjects and of incomplete commentaries on the Bible and on the Qur'ān. His advanced views on religious questions roused much opposition among his co-religionists, though they also met with some support. In 1862 he founded the Scientific Society, and in 1872 started the *Tahzīb ul Akhlāq*, a magazine through which he exerted his greatest influence. It met with many difficulties, being twice given up and restarted before finally ceasing publication. In the first period of its activity, seven years, it printed 226 articles, of which 112 were by Sir Sayyid. He wrote good, flowing and simple Urdu, discarding the florid style of his predecessors in journalism. The artificial style had such a hold on Urdu writers that his book, *Āṣār us Sanādīd*, was first put into literary form by Imām Bakhsh Ṣahbāī, the well-known writer of ornate Urdu, and it was only at a later date that Sir Sayyid ventured to write it himself in his own natural, simple style. Other magazines were started to oppose his. They were sometimes written in the very style

which they were condemning—the earnestness of the authors made them natural in spite of themselves. For a time the issue of the conflict seemed doubtful, but ultimately, so far as prose went, he won a complete victory, and no one now thinks of writing in the style of Surūr when he has before him as a model the forceful and straightforward writing of Sir Sayyid. The men who best understood his spirit and most faithfully followed his principles were Alṭāf Ḥusain Ḥalī and Vaḥīd ud Dīn Salīm. (See Nos. 218, 230.)

213. Gulām Gauṣ Bekhabar (1824–1905) was born in Lhasa and brought up in Benares. Most of his life was spent in Government service. His *Khānāba e Jigar* is in Persian verse, but he has left an Urdu work, *Figān i Bekhabar* (1891) which is sometimes quoted as *Figān i Beṣabr*. He was a very good letter-writer.

The influence of Fort William was in the direction of simplicity. But the love for an ornate, artificial style was so great that at first this simple method of writing was scoffed at. Surūr in his *Fasāna e 'Ajāib* wrote against Mīr Amman. In spite of mockery it conquered. It was assisted by the tracts and books produced by religious writers like Sayyid Aḥmad, the Vahābī (not the same as Sir Sayyid Aḥmad), his disciple 'Abdullāh in *Tanbīh ul Gāfilīn* (translated from a Persian book written by his master Sayyid Aḥmad), Gulām Imām Shahīd, and Ḥājī Isma'īl in *Taqviyyat ul Imān*. Delhi, at first in opposition, soon accepted the natural style; the objections of Lucknow took much longer to overcome. In 1832 Urdu became the language of the law courts, many legal terms were introduced, and thus the language was strengthened in a new direction. The primary and secondary schools, by their demand for simple textbooks gave a further stimulus to the movement towards simplicity. Finally, Sir Sayyid Aḥmad threw the whole weight of his influence on to the same side.

214. Amīr Aḥmad Mīnāī (1828–1900) is better known as a poet (No. 178). He published a volume of letters written in very smooth, good Urdu. His *Intikhāb i Yādgār*, an anthology of 410 poets connected with Rāmpūr, has introductions written in the ornate style which we associate with Surūr. By order of Vājid 'Alī Shāh he wrote *Hidāyat us Sulṭān*

and *Irshād us Sulṭān*, which brought him great fame. He can hardly be said to be a writer of literary prose.

215. MUḤAMMAD ḤUSAIN ĀZĀD (d. 1910), professor of Arabic in the Government College, Lahore, is by some regarded as the greatest of Urdu prose writers. He wrote in a very agreeable, picturesque style, using a good many expressive Hindi words, yet here and there introducing an unfamiliar Arabic or Persian one. There is nothing flamboyant in his writing. He often stages his thoughts in a poetical manner, but he does not attempt rhyming words or rhythmical constructions. His Urdu Reading Books, the Primer and First, Second, and Third Books, show an amazing ability to write the simplest Urdu in the most charming way. His volume, *Qiṣaṣ i Hind*, stories of Indian history, is another example of this.

His most famous work is *Āb i Ḥayāt*, a history of Urdu poetry. It can hardly be described as scientific; he accepted too readily what had been said by others and relied too much on his prodigious memory. Some of his accounts of people's lives, and statements about books which have since been published, are now known to be inaccurate. The book contained little literary criticism, but it led the way and as a pioneer work deserves our respect. Another important book is his edition of the poems of his teacher Ẕauq. His *Darbār i Akbarī* is a large historical work. He was a great Persian scholar, and apart from Persian Readers for schools he wrote two histories of Persian literature, *Sukhandān i Fārs* and *Nigāristān i Fārs*. His *Nairang i Khayāl* is an allegorical study.

He made his influence felt in education, journalism and literature; his great accomplishment lay in what he did for prose by his inimitable style, and for poetry by introducing along with Ḥālī the new era of thought. (See No. 232.)

216. CIRĀG ʿALĪ (1844–95) was a well-known civil servant whose latter days were spent in Ḥaidarābād. Apart from one or two Government reports his work consists almost entirely of controversial and other religious books or tracts. His letters, *Majmūʿa e Rasāil*, deserve mention.

217. MUSHTĀQ ḤUSAIN VAQĀR UL MULK (1839–1917) had

a career similar to that of Cirāg ʿAlī. He worked first in British India and afterwards in Ḥaidarābād. He wrote for *Tahẕīb ul Aḵẖlāq* on social ,and religious reform, and translated two books on France. He had a good command of virile Urdu, but was too fond of big Arabic words.

218. **Hali.** ALṬĀF ḤUSAIN ḤĀLĪ (1837–1914), the great contemporary and friend of Āzād, was famous both as poet and as prose writer. He wrote three large volumes of biography, *Ḥayāt i Jāved*, a life of Sir Sayyid Aḥmad, perhaps his greatest prose work; *Yādgār i Gālib*, a life of Gālib; and *Ḥayāt i Saʿdī*, a life of the Persian poet Saʿdī. In the field of poetics he wrote *Shiʿr o Shāʿirī*, 199 pages long, a valuable introduction to his *Dīvān*; in this he discusses the different varieties of Urdu poetry. Among his minor works are *Tiryāq i Masmūm* (1868), a religious controversial book; *Majlis un Nisā* (1874) and *Maqālāt i Ḥālī*, a collection of magazine articles, contributed chiefly to *Tahẕīb ul Aḵẖlāq*. (See No. 231.)

Ḥālī's style is free from artificial ornament, a little monotonous, yet straightforward and vigorous, as is seen when he writes on scientific subjects. Sometimes it is really good, but his informality displeased readers. It is remarkable that he and Āzād, the pioneers of the new movement in Urdu literature, which owed so much to English influence, were themselves indifferent English scholars.

219. **Muhsin ul Mulk.** SAYYID MAHDĪ ʿALĪ, MUḤSIN UL MULK (1837–1907) was a friend of Sir Sayyid Aḥmad, whose views he advocated by numerous articles in *Tahẕīb ul Aḵẖlāq*. He exercised a great influence in Ḥaidarābād, where he was employed after some years of Government service, and was largely instrumental in getting Urdu recognised as the State language. His writings have been collected into a number of volumes. They deal chiefly with subjects of special interest to Muslims, and their life and religion. His books include collections of lectures, magazine articles and letters.

220. **Shibli.** SHIBLĪ NUʿMĀNĪ (1857–1914) was a voluminous writer on historical, religious and literary subjects. His most important contributions to the history of Islām are his biographies, *Sīrat un Nuʿmān*, *Al Fārūq*, *Al Gazzālī*,

Sīrat un Nabī in three volumes, *Al Māmūn*, *Sawānih i Maulānā Rūm*. His chief works on literary subjects are *Muāzina e Anīs o Dabīr*, *Shi'r ul 'Ajam* and *Bayān i Khusrau*. The first of these, the *Muāzina*, compared Anis and Dabir to the advantage of Anis; a reply by Fauq called *Al Mīzān* advocated the claims of Dabir. *Shi'r ul 'Ajam* is a history of Persian poetry in five volumes. His *Safarnāma e Miṣr o Rūm o Shām* is a book of travel, describing his journeys in Egypt, Turkey and Syria. He wrote several books of poetry which are much inferior to his prose work. In addition to these he published collections of letters, articles and lectures.

Some people consider him the greatest of Urdu prose writers. His style is stately and literary, occasionally stiff, but brighter than Ḥāli's. It is well adapted to the religious and historical subjects with which he dealt. He avoids prolixity and exaggeration, yet sometimes he repeats the same idea over and over again in different words. At one time he gave great assistance to the Nadvat ul 'Ulamā, an institution for the study of Muslim theology and history; later on he founded in A'ẓamgaṛh the Dār ul Muṣannifīn or Shiblī Academy. Its chief object was the study of Muslim literature, especially Arabic, Persian and Urdu. In this connection it devoted special attention to the collection of MSS.

The Three Novelists—Nazir Ahmad, Sarshar and Sharar. At the end of the century these three men were writing novels of very different types. Naẕir Aḥmad wrote domestic novels, chiefly for women and girls, and advocated the reform of life in the Muslim home; Sarshār gave himself to vivid, humorous and sparkling description of ordinary Lucknow life; he had no religious end in view. Sharar's historical novels were written to depict the past glories of Islām in Spain, Arabia, Persia and India.

221. Naẕir Aḥmad (1831–1912) was essentially a reformer. While ardently attached to his own faith he was not a bigot; he felt the need for a pure practical religion and civilised domestic life. In *Taubat un Naṣūḥ* he wrote of religious repentance, in *Banāt un Na'sh* and *Mirāt ul 'Arūs* of daily home life, in *Rūyā e Ṣādiqa* and *Cand Pand* of

religious beliefs and practices. In *Muḥṣanāt* he preached monogamy, and in *'Ayyāmā* he advocated the re-marriage of widows. In addition to these he showed his mastery over Urdu by his translations of the Indian Penal Code, the Income Tax Act and the Indian Evidence Act. He translated the Qur'ān into excellent Urdu and published the translation without the Arabic text, an unusual thing among Muḥammadans. He wrote several books on the Qur'ān and Muslim religious duties; in later life he lectured a good deal, and some of his lectures were published. Under the name of Benagīr he wrote some verse of no poetic merit, but interesting in the fact that much of it deals with nature subjects.

His easy familiar style, carefully altered to fit his characters, is well suited to his novels, which have great literary value. But it is not so well fitted for religious works, where some of his colloquialisms seem undignified; even his translation of the Qur'ān is not free from them. Though he was a learned Arabic scholar he generally avoids obtruding his knowledge of Arabic. His chief title to fame lies in his having founded a new school of novelists and a new kind of novel—the domestic novel. He has a worthy successor in Rāshid ul Khairī. A gentle vein of humour runs through his stories, but it never comes much to the surface.

222. RATN NĀTH SARSHĀR (1846–1902) was a humorist and novelist. To understand his literary position we must remember that he was a journalist; his most famous book, *Fasāna e Āzād*, a novel of enormous length, appeared in his paper, the *Avadh Akhbār*, and has all the faults of hasty work done from day to day. As a description lively and gay, often broadly farcical, of all conceivable characters in all ranks of society to be seen in the Vanity Fair of Lucknow it is inimitable, but we do not find in it any carefully worked-out plot or delineation of character. He was casual, lazy and careless. For a long time he would remain idle, then he would dash off a few chapters. In that way he did nearly all his work. His novels, *Hushshū*, *Pī Kahān*, *Bichṛī Dulhan*, *Ṭūfān i Betamīzī and Kaṛam Dhum*, have the same rollicking fun and insouciance running through all of them.

In addition to novels and a little poetry, which is not devoid of merit, he translated with great success several works from English, such as Wallace's *Russia* and Dufferin's *Letters from High Latitudes*; his novel, *Khudāī Faujdār*, is an adaptation of Don Quixote. Sarshār uses the idiomatic Urdu of Lucknow; there is a ceaseless flow of conversational idioms, the language of the man in the street; there is no stiffness or halting in anything he writes; he is intensely human and his pictures are full of life. Rajab 'Alī Beg Surūr, who described Lucknow life a generation earlier, leaves the impression of a dream; Sarshār's pictures on the other hand are vividly real, his style entirely natural and unartificial.

223. 'Abd ul Ḥalīm Sharar (1860–1926) was a journalist, historian and novelist. He wrote chiefly historical novels about the old days of Islām in different countries, but one or two deal with modern life in India. Their fundamental idea comes from Scott's *Waverley Novels*. They number about 30 in all; the best known perhaps are *Mansūr-Mohana*, *Ḥasan aur Anjalīna*, *Firdaus i Barīn* and *Malik 'Azīz aur Varjana*. They differ little from one another, the same heroes and heroines under varying names appear in them all; the same sudden attachments and conversions occur over and over again. They are mere stories, not historical studies. He does not recreate the spirit of the country or people of whom he writes, and in all his novels he is intensely solemn; none of his characters ever laugh, at the same time they are interesting, and through much fighting, plotting and secrecy the reader is carried on to the necessary conclusion.

He wrote a large number of books dealing with the early history of Islām and its heroes; and was sometimes involved in fierce controversy. He wrote ceaselessly for the press, started several magazines which enjoyed only a brief existence, and delivered many lectures. His life was one of great activity. His style is plain and unadorned, rising to greater vigour in his historical and social writings, especially his magazine articles, than in his novels.

224. Muḥammad Ẕakā Ullāh (1832–1910) was an educationist whose work was mostly translation and com-

pilation. He had a good, but not exalted, style and his translations read as if they were originals. He was interested mainly in mathematics and history. His most important historical works are a *History of India* in many volumes, *The British Period of Indian History*, *Āīn i Qaiṣarī* (the Victorian period), and a *Life of Lord Curzon*.

225. Imām Bakhsh Ṣahbāī (d. 1857) was another educationist who had a great reputation as a writer of Urdu in the old ornate style. As we have seen above he wrote Sir Sayyid Aḥmad's *Āṣār i Sanādīd* in this style before Sir Sayyid himself wrote it in simple and direct Urdu. He was killed at the time of the Mutiny.

226. Sajjād Ḥusain (1856–1915) was a novelist of some distinction. In 1877 he began the issue of *Avadh Punch* and he himself was the first editor. His chief novels are *Ṭilismī Fānūs*, *Ṭarhdār Laundī*, *Kāyā Palaṭ*, *Mīṭhī Churī*, *Ḥājī Bagol* and *Pyārī Dunyā*. His style was fresh and pleasing with plenty of life and humour.

227. Sayyid Aḥmad of Delhi (1846 to c. 1920) was the author of a number of educational works chiefly for women and girls, and also of dictionaries and other works, including one or two stories. His most important publication is his famous Urdu dictionary, *Farhang i Āṣafīya* (1892).

228. Sayyid 'Alī Bilgrāmī (1851–1911) is known for two important translations, *Tamaddun i 'Arab* from Le Bon's book on the civilisation of the Arabs, and *Tamaddun i Hind*, the civilisation of India.

229. Ṣafīr Bilgrāmī (1833–?) was not related to the foregoing. He lived a large part of his life in Āra and wrote much verse, principally love lyrics. His published books include an anthology, *Ṣalawāt i Khiẓr*, and volumes of lyrics called *Safīr i Bulbul* and *Khumkhāna e Safīr*. He wrote a novel, *Rūḥ Afzā*, which was not published. Perhaps his most important work was *Jalva e Khiẓr*, a history of Urdu literature, which he wrote with a view to correcting what he considered the mis-statements of Āzād's *Āb i Ḥayāt*.

230. Vaḥīd ud Dīn Salīm of Pānīpat (d. 1928) was Professor of Urdu in the Osmania University, Ḥaidarābād. He was a follower and friend of Sir Sayyid Aḥmad, and

worked in his spirit. Along with ʿAbd ul Ḥaqq, secretary of the Anjuman i Taraqqi e Urdū, he was leader of the Hindi movement in Urdu, and in this connection he wrote the remarkable book, *Vaẓaʿ e Iṣṭilaḥāt*, on the formation of technical terms in Urdu.

VII

THE NEW AGE

WE have seen how Urdu poetry became enslaved to Persian models, with the result that the life passed out of it, and it became artificial and insincere. Outward expression, mere cleverness of phraseology or thought, was everything; inner beauty, artless simplicity of idea and true seriousness were absent. To a large extent this is the case even to-day, but a great change has made itself felt; side by side with the old, a new school of thought and poetry has arisen and is freeing Urdu from the shackles of the past and leading it into poetic truth and earnestness. This is chiefly the result of English influence, through education and literature.

The pioneers of the new school were Alṭaf Ḥusain Ḥālī and Muḥammad Ḥusain Āzād. By a fortunate circumstance they found themselves in Lahore at the same time, working in the Education Department, at the head of which was Col. Holroyd, a man of sympathetic spirit. At his instigation they inaugurated in 1874 poetical gatherings in which poems were recited that expressed the new ideas. In spite of considerable opposition the work was begun and the new era ushered in. Urdu poetry definitely entered upon a new stage. The leaders avoided two dangers, the Scylla of artificial insincerity on which most Urdu poetry down to that time had suffered shipwreck, and the Charybdis of exaggerated westernisation into which some of the younger writers fell in the end of the nineteenth century.

231. **Hali.** ALṬĀF ḤUSAIN ḤĀLĪ of Pānīpat (1837–1914) went to Delhi as a young man. After the Mutiny he entered the service of the poet and critic, Shefta, whose pupil he became. He also received much help from Ġālib. These two men, especially Shefta, influenced him greatly in poetical

matters. Still greater was the influence of English books, which he read while working under Col. Holroyd. In the poetical meetings of 1874 and 1875 he read some of the poems by which he was to become famous, poems which marked him out as a pioneer. Such were *Ḥubb i Vaṭn*, *Raḥm o Inṣāf*, *Nishāṭ i Ummed* and *Barkhā Rut*. These poems and others like them show beautiful simplicity and directness of thought, and really attempt to express truth.

The influence of Sir Sayyid Aḥmad turned his attention to the spiritual uplift of his co-religionists. This found fruit in his longest poem, *Madd o Jazr i Islām*, commonly known as the *Musaddas i Ḥālī*, which with its appendix is 2,800 lines long. It is a glowing account of the former glories of Islām, a lament over its decadent condition and a trumpet call to reform. No single poem has had so great an effect on the Urdu-speaking world. The spirit of reform is shown also in his short poems about women, *Bewā kī Munājāt*, *Cup kī Dād* and *Shikwa e Hind* and in the elegies on the death of his friends, Gālib, Maḥmūd Khān and Sir Sayyid Aḥmad. The *Musaddas* is his greatest poem, and next to this come the short poems just mentioned, which are very popular. He published also two volumes of poetry, *Dīwān i Ḥālī* and *Majmū'a e Naẓm i Ḥālī*. In his *Musaddas* he shows real power; the mind is swept along by enthusiasm for the past with sorrow over what has been lost. Some say he exaggerates; but the need for reform is ever present, and the stirrings of the soul reaching out to better things are a tribute to the force of his appeal. It is the greatest Urdu poem since the time of Anīs. Ḥālī is in the first rank of Urdu poets. (See No. 218.)

THE ANCIENT GLORIES OF ARABIA

From Ḥālī's *Musaddas*

In those dark days no elegance of speech
   Was known; the paths of eloquence were sealed;
The literature of Rome had ceased to be,
   And Persia's old religion was no more—
When suddenly Arabia's lightning blazed,
   And every man was smitten wide awake.

And when they knew the Arabs' flaming words,
And plainly heard the fashion of their speech,
And felt the verses racing through their veins,
Their sermons rushing like a stream in flood,
Those magic phrases, charmèd sentences,
Then they perceived themselves but dumb before;

They had not known how they might praise or blame,
Nor how express their sadness or their joy,
Nor how give sacred counsel or command—
Treasure of tongue and pen was buried, lost.
Now Arabs taught them tuneful melodies,
Arabia's speech unloosed the tongues of men.

THE PRESENT EVIL CONDITION OF ISLAM IN INDIA

From Ḥālī's *Musaddas*

The race whose step was firm on every land,
Whose banner waved in all the winds of heaven,
People whose honour all horizons knew—
"The best of nations" was their title proud—
Nothing remains of that proud folk but this,
That we still give ourselves the Muslim name.

For otherwise within our veins and blood,
In our intentions and our search for truth,
Our hearts and minds and thoughts and tongues and speech,
Our nature, habits, dispositions too,
Remains there nought of old nobility,—
Or if there be, it is by chance alone.

For now our every deed ignoble shows,
Our actions are the meanest of the low;
The fair name of our fathers is eclipsed;
Our very steps disgrace the place we dwell.
Dishonoured is the honour of the past,
Arabia's greatness sunk beyond recall.

232. **Azad.** Muḥammad Ḥusain Āzād (c. 1834–1910), who has been dealt with more fully under prose writers (No. 215), is important also as a poet, particularly because he was a pioneer. His poetic output was small; indeed, not 5,000 lines of his have been published. He presided over the first meeting of the poetic assembly in 1874, delivered a lecture and read a poem, *Shab i Qadr*. In the early days he did even more than Ḥālī to introduce the new views. Though the meetings ceased within a year, it was impossible to stem the tide. Others threw in their lot with Āzād and

Ḥālī, and in spite of checks from time to time, the movement grew in strength. Āzād's poetry is in one small volume called *Nazm i Āzād*. It contains a number of poems on subjects like Love of Country, Dawn of Hope, Night, and the Dream of Peace, some love lyrics of less value, and a few odes. Like Ḥālī he deplored conventional exaggeration and strove to be natural, to express in forceful language the feelings which animated him, and to describe what he saw. He would be better known as a poet if he were not so famous as a prose writer.

233. MUḤAMMAD ISMĀ'ĪL (1844–1917) belonged to Meraṭh and worked in the Education Department, for which he wrote books. He gave his support to the new school and always kept the new ideas before him. His poetry has been printed in one volume, *Kulliyāt i Ismā'īl*, which contains a large number of short poems. Two of them are in blank verse. He wrote on everyday subjects with great directness and simplicity, avoiding the defects of the old style. Shiblī had a very high opinion of him and put him after Ḥālī among the poets of the new school. As a prose-writer he is known by a number of excellent Urdu readers which have been used with success in the lower classes of schools.

234. **Akbar.** AKBAR ḤUSAIN RIẒVĪ AKBAR (1846-1921), named Lisān ul 'Aṣr, Mouthpiece of the Age, is the last but one of the front-rank Urdu poets. He spent many years in Government service, and on retirement in 1903 devoted himself to literature. He belonged to the new school, though at first he wrote in the old style. He was a fervent patriot, who preached love not only for his religion but for the East as a whole with its customs and peoples. He published three volumes of letters, valuable as examples of good prose, and three volumes of poems, each called *Kulliyāt*. His chief characteristic is his use of humour and satire to enforce his views on national, political and social subjects; in this he was both effective and popular. His command of pure Urdu, his ability to bend to his purpose strange words, whether English or vernacular, his appeal to his countrymen, both Hindu and Muslim, both learned and unlearned, his humour and his wit, his flow of language and

charm of style, mark him out as a writer of eminence. He was a master of moral, didactic and political verse.

235. **Surur.** Durgā Sahāe Surūr (1873–1910), usually known as Surūr Jahānābādi, is one of the most remarkable of recent poets. His life was sad; to secure a living he sold fugitive verses to anyone who would buy them. Happily two volumes of poems have been preserved, *Jām i Surūr* and *Khumkhāna e Surūr*. He disliked the unreal images and meaningless expressions of the old poetry, and did not care for love lyrics, but, like Naẓīr of Āgra (No. 125), delighted in everyday subjects. He was an Indian first and foremost; being a Hindu he was able to enter into a phase of Indian life little touched on except by Qulī Quṭb Shāh (No. 20) and Naẓīr. He loved the old heroes, and the stories of Hindu life and religion; his poems are full of national sentiment.

He was specially fond of nature-subjects and those which brought out the inherent tenderness of his character; his imagination was vivid, and his command of language great. He liked simplicity and preferred vernacular Hindi words to those taken from Arabic and Persian. He never had a poetical teacher and was therefore free from the fetters that bound many of his fellow poets. Urdu poetry suffered a great loss in his premature death.

236. Nādir ʿAlī Khān Nādir (1867–1912) is another prominent name in the new movement. He was a much better English scholar than Surūr and shows more western influence in his writing. He was a patriotic writer, but wrote more on imaginative subjects than on the things of everyday life.

237. Muḥammad Muḥsin Muḥsin (1825–1905), called Kākauravī after his native village, was a lawyer who gave his leisure time to literature. At first he wrote odes and love lyrics but he gave them up for *naʿt*, praise of Muḥammad, in which he gained great fame. He and Amīr Mīnāī are the best writers of this kind of poetry. He was a friendly man of old fashioned courtesy. In verse he combined high sounding words with fertility of ideas, happy metaphors and allusions to well known stories.

238. Aḥmad ʿAlī Shauq Qidvāī, is one of the chief poets

of the last 50 years. He wrote simple and beautiful poems on nature and love, such as *Tarāna e Shauq*, *Ganjīna*, *Nairang i Jamāl*, *'Ālam i Khayāl*; also the plays, *Macpherson aur Lucy* and *Qāsim o Zuhra*. In his revolt against artificial ornament and Persian constructions he did a real service to the language.

239. 'Alī Muḥammad Shād of Patna, who died in 1927, for many years took part in all the life of his city. He was a prolific writer, very fond of writing congratulatory odes and other poems on occasions of public or domestic importance. He is the author of many elegies which are noteworthy for their freedom from exaggeration. His poetry suffered from haste and over-production, for he gave no time to revision and correction.

240. 'Aẓmat Ullāh Khān of Delhi (d. 1927) must be mentioned chiefly on account of his resolutely turning to Hindi models in language, thought and metres. Some think that in this respect he will have a great, even an epoch-making influence on Urdu poetry. Though not a poet of the first rank, he is well worth reading. He wrote in a rather feminine style.

VIII

CONCLUSION

We have now come to the end of our survey of Urdu Literature. In dealing with English influence we have spoken of the work of Fort William College in the beginning of the ninteenth century; Col. Holroyd and his connection with Ḥālī and Āzād have been referred to on p. 94 in explanation of the characteristics of the New Age. Mention should also be made of the Delhi College, 1827–57, to which Sir Sayyid Aḥmad, Naẕīr Aḥmad, Zakā Ullāh and Ẓiyā ud Dīn owed so much. English influence is seen in the increased attention paid to thought and matter as opposed to language and form, in more naturalness and less conventionality, and, generally, in greater breadth of subject and treatment. Going more into detail, we may note the following as due to it.

(*a*) Study of nature. Formerly descriptions of nature were largely conventional and artificial. Exceptions may be found in Qulī Quṭb Shāh, Naẕīr of Agra, and Durgā Sahāe Surūr. Naẕīr Aḥmad, No. 221, wrote many nature poems, but he is little esteemed as a poet. Other students of nature were Ḥālī, Āzād, Ismā'īl, Akbar, Shauq Qidvāī and Iqbāl.

(*b*) The same writers are prominent in poetry of description. They write of flowers, insects, birds and other living creatures, occasionally of festivals and famous buildings.

(*c*) Another form of poetry which owes its inspiration largely to English sources is that which breathes love of country and true patriotism, portraying the glories and beauties of scenes and events loved by the author, but not decrying or belittling other lands and peoples.

(*d*) Moral and didactic verse has much increased in popularity of recent years; its poetic value is not great, but its ethical value is enormous. Indian opinion has eagerly availed itself of the support given by English literature, and the difference in moral tone between Urdu writings of today and those of days gone by is almost beyond telling. Indeed, the sympathy between the best sentiment in India and the great writers in England, particularly in moral aspirations, is a happy augury for the days to come.

Religious poetry, when, as in Hālī's *Musaddas*, it is free from bigotry, helps to this end, for it then rouses men to a realisation of all that is best in them, including love for others.

(*c*) As regards poetical form and language, Urdu has not changed much under English influence. There was a time, a few years ago, when it appeared likely to adopt many western models, but it has not done so, and it remains nearly as it was. This dislike of change has encouraged the continuance of over-Persianisation (which, as we have seen, is one of the greatest hindrances to the true development of Urdu poetry), and has prevented the employment of new forms of verse.

Prose has made more advance than poetry in the last twenty-five years. It is less shackled by convention, and though it suffers from the blight of Persian and Arabic, which eat out its vitality, it is freer and more vigorous than all but a small part of the poetry. Novels are becoming more and more numerous, but no great novelist has yet arisen, one capable of delineating growth of character and developing a plot. Prem Cand, who writes both Urdu and Hindi, nearly achieved greatness in this respect, before he gave up his short stories, which were admirable, for his long novels, which are unconvincing and improbable. He will never attain the heights which are within his reach unless he goes back to his tales of the village life which he has lived, and the Hindu villagers whom he understands. Those tales alone ring true, and only they enable him to express his soul.

The range of Urdu poetry is still very circumscribed. We have seen that epics can hardly be said to exist, the only substitutes being the elegies relating to Karbalā (p. 61). There is no dramatic poetry. Plays are being written in ever-increasing numbers, but they are not literature. If the Urdu writers of today would make a study of Shakespeare, Milton, Tennyson and Browning, they might create a whole new world for their readers.

In prose we miss philosophy, impartial history and penetrating criticism. There are works on historical subjects, but generally speaking they show a lack of genuine research and unprejudiced investigation. Criticism tends to confine itself to questions of verbal cleverness and linguistic correctness. Little or no effort is made to discuss an author's thoughts and meaning, or estimate his poetry as a whole, and when lines are quoted from his poems, we are not told in what poem they occur or when they were written. We must, however, recognise a certain improvement of late, which gives encouragement for the future. Many of the Urdu magazines, which are now numerous, are devoted to literary subjects, and the level of criticism is getting higher.

About 250 authors have been mentioned in this work. Apart from Prem Cand, who has just been alluded to, only eight are Hindus, the rest are Muhammadans. The eight are Nos. 18, 132, 192, 193, 198, 210, 222 and 235. The only famous writers among them are Dayā Shankar Nasīm, Ratn Nāth Sarshār and Durgā Sahāe Surūr. Hindu authors of real ability prefer to write in Hindi. To explain the situation we may liken Urdu, with its Hindi, Persian and Arabic elements, to English, with Anglo-Saxon, Latin and Greek. Hindi, and especially Sanskritised Hindi, is what English would be if we excluded words of Latin and Greek origin and introduced Anglo-Saxon, while Urdu corresponds to English with an excess of Latin and Greek words. Hindi is written in Sanskrit letters, Urdu in adapted Arabic letters. Again, Sanskrit is the sacred language of Hindus, Arabic of Muhammadans. Instead of having one strong, virile language for both communities, we find two languages, rendered stiff and almost unintelligible by the over-use of Sanskrit in one and Persian or Arabic in the other.

It is perhaps an illustration of the need for female education that there are no women in the list, though we saw on p. 28 that Princess Khadija was a great patron of letters, and on p. 25 that a lady in Sidhoṭ had ordered a copy of *Phulban* from Rustumī.

The future of Urdu depends chiefly on the great mass of its speakers and writers, but also on the Osmaniya University in Ḥaidarābād; to some extent, too, on the Anjuman i Taraqqī e Urdū, with its headquarters in Aurangābād, and the Hindustānī Academy. Connected with the University is the Dār ut Tarjuma, a translation bureau which exists for the purpose of familiarising the Urdu reading public with scientific work in Europe, and especially in Great Britain. The Anjuman is purely literary, and, under the guidance of its secretary, ʿAbd ul Ḥaqq, Professor of Urdu in the Osmaniya University, serves the interests of Urdu literature by the issue of its quarterly magazine, *Urdū*, and the production of books, old and new. It is related to the Muḥammadan Educational Conference, which is a product of ʿAlīgaṛh University. The Hindustānī Academy, under the auspices of Government, has two branches, Hindi and Urdu, the members being exclusively Indians. Two quarterly magazines are published, one for each language, and valuable work is being done. In addition to these institutions there is the Shiblī Academy in Aʿẓamgaṛh, which endeavours to give to India not only the best of Muslim thought, but also the philosophy of the west, and thus in some measure to supply a want which has been referred to above.

We have hitherto not referred to living authors except incidentally, but it seems fitting to give some account of one who occupies a place among the great Urdu poets.

241. **Iqbal.** Sir Muḥammad Iqbāl (1875–) is a Panjabi. He was born in Siālkoṭ, where he received his education till he reached manhood. He took his degree in Lahore. From 1905 to 1908 he was in England and Germany. These years in the west left a permanent mark upon his life and thought. He has written in both Persian and Urdu, but for some time now has devoted himself to philosophical subjects and has not written verse.

His first poem, *Ode to the Himalayas*, was written in 1901. At one time he wished to give up poetry, but on Sir Thomas Arnold's advice, took it up again. His poetical writings show excessive Persian influence, which unfortunately is most clearly seen in his latest poems.

His best work is contained in *Bāng i Dirā*, 1924, which is divided into three parts according to date—(i) before, (ii) during, and (iii) after, his visit to Europe, 1905–8. He is fond of nature subjects, such as flowers and animals, the moon, the stars and the clouds, evening and night, the banks of the Rāvī and the mountains. All his poems are short. The best known are *Khiẓr i Rāh*, *Taṣvīr i Dard*, *Shikva*, *Javāb i Shikva*, and his *Odes to the Himalayas*, *to Golkunḍā*, *to the Firefly* and *to the Cloud*.

He sings the praises of Muslim achievement, for he is not a national but a Muslim patriot, one who has imbibed some of the culture of the West, but holds himself rather aloof, not so much antagonistic to it as suspicious of its effects on his co-religionists. Like Hālī, he looks back to a golden age, but he feels a greater personal pain at its passing away. Latterly he appears to have experienced much disillusionment and become somewhat embittered. However, as he has hardly passed his prime, he may once again write poetry, and he may then be able to view the world with greater optimism. Some of his admirers have named him Tarjumān i Ḥaqīqat, Interpreter of the Truth.

BIBLIOGRAPHY

BOOKS ON URDU LITERATURE

The following books are known to the writer personally. From this list are excluded Persian anthologies, books dealing with individual poets, and volumes of poetry, whether with or without an introduction.

URDU BOOKS

1. *Āb i Ḥayāt*. By M. Ḥusain Āzād. 556 pp. c. 1880. A bright chatty account in beautiful Urdu of 70 poets down to 1875; contains many amusing stories; about 200 pp. of quotations from *gazals*; historical order.

2. *Gul i Ra'nā*. By 'Abd ul Ḥai Nadavī. 545 pp. 1925. A long introduction on the course of Urdu poetry, mentioning a few better-known Dakhnī poets; account of seven Dakhnī and 63 north Indian poets; historical order.

3. *Khumkhāna e Jāved*. By Srī Rām. 4 vols., 2,550 pp. In alphabetical order of takhallus, dealing with 2,054 versifiers; completed down to the letter *shīn*, the last name being Shu'ūr. Many biographical details, but little about poems or style; if completed will comprise about 4,600 pp., and contain notices of about 4,000 writers. First volume out of print.

4. *Shi'r ul Hind*. By 'Abd us Salām Nadavī. 2 vols., 907 pp. c. 1926. Vol. I deals with selected poets in historical order; Vol. II speaks of different kinds of poetry and the men who wrote it. Both vols. have copious quotations.

5. *Āb i Baqā*. By Ja'far 'Ali Nishtar. 280 pp. 1918. Tells of 25 poets chosen at random, and has a chapter on Rāmpūr.

6. *Siyar ul Muṣannifīn*. By M. Yaḥyā Tanhā. 2 vols. 879 pp. 1924 and 1928. On Urdu prose writers from 1798 to present day; long biographical account of later writers,

refers to their chief works, and quotes from some. Very few recent writers mentioned.

7. *Maḥbūb uz Zaman*. By ʻAbd ul Jabbār Khān Āṣafī, 2 vols., 1,242 pp. c. 1870. Out of print. Deals with Dakhni poets; much biographical detail, but little about poetry.

8. *Urdū e Qadīm*. By Shams Ullāh Qādrī. 158 pp. 1927. Useful information about early writers and the early history of Urdu.

9. *Dakan meṉ Urdū*. By Naṣīr ud Dīn Hāshimī. 332 pp. 1926. Like the last mentioned.

10. *Urdū ke Asālīb i Bayān*. By Gulām Muḥiyyud Dīn Qādrī. 204 pp. 1927. A clever book on selected prose writers and their style; does not mention their works.

11. *Arbāb i Nasr*. By Sayyid Muḥammad. 306 pp. 1927. On the early Urdu translators connected with Fort William College, Calcutta.

12. *Panjāb meṉ Urdū*. By Maḥmūd Shīrānī. 327 pp. 1928. Much interesting material. Claims a high place for the Panjāb in the development of Urdu from early times to the present day.

13. *Shiʻr o Shāʻirī*. By Alṭāf Ḥusain Ḥālī. 197 pp. 1896. Monograph on Urdu poetic style and various kinds of poetry.

14. *Hamārī Shāʻirī*. By Masʻūd Ḥasan Riẓvī. 132 pp. 1928. Sketchy essays in defence of Urdu poetry.

15. *Tanqīdī Miqālāt*. By author of No. 10. Essays in criticism with illustrative critiques.

16. *Urdū Shahpāre*. By author of No. 10. 365 pp. 1929. Urdu literature to the time of Valī; copious, well chosen extracts; a valuable book.

17. *Dunyā e Afsāna*. By ʻAbd ul Qādir Sarvarī. 215 pp. 1927.

English and French Books

18. *Histoire de la Littérature Hindouie et Hindoustanie*. By Garcin de Tassy. 3 vols., 1,840 pp. 1870. Founded on Persien and Urdu anthologies; in alphabetic order; deals with Urdu and Hindi writers and shows amazing industry for one who had never been in India.

19. *History of Urdu Literature*. By Rām Bābū Saksena.

385 pp. 1927. A good but discursive account; very useful to those who cannot read Urdu.

20. *Influence of English Literature on Urdu Literature.* By 'Abd ul Laṭīf. 146 pp. 1924. Brightly written from the new standpoint; a good deal of information.

21. *Catalogue of Hindustani MSS. in the Library of the India Office.* By James Fuller Blumhardt. 183 pp. 1926. Many useful biographical details.

22. *Hindustani Literature;* in the *Encyclopaedia Britannica* (9th Edition, Vol. XI, pp. 843 ff.). By Sir C. J. Lyall. A brief account of Hindi and Urdu literature.

SYSTEM OF TRANSLITERATION OF URDU LETTERS

Urdu Alphabet	Representation by Roman character	Urdu Alphabet	Representation by Roman character	Urdu Alphabet	Representation by Roman character
ب	b	ذ	z̤	غ	g̠
پ	p	ر	r	ف	f
ت	t	ڑ	ṛ	ق	q
ٹ	ṭ	ز	z	ک	k
ث	s̤	ژ	zh	گ	g
ج	j	س	s	ل	l
چ	c	ش	sh	م	m
ح	ḥ	ص	ṣ	ن	n
خ	kh	ض	ẓ	و	v
د	d	ط	ṭ	ه	h
ڈ	ḍ	ظ	ẓ	ي	y
		ع	ʻ	*nasal vowel*	ãṉ, eṉ, *etc.*

INDEX OF PERSONS

In each case entered under the best-known name. The first number given is the consecutive number, when there is one; the numerals following refer to pages. K.=Khan; M.=Muhammad.

INDEX OF WORKS

(Only real names are entered)

INDEX OF SUBJECTS